THE
BRONZE AGE
COMPUTER DISC

THE
BRONZE AGE
COMPUTER DISC

ALAN BUTLER

quantum

LONDON • NEW YORK • TORONTO • SYDNEY

quantum

An imprint of W. Foulsham & Co. Ltd.
The Publishing House, Bennetts Close,
Cippenham, Slough, Berkshire, SL1 5AP, England

Photographs on pages 14 and 15 courtesy of
the Hellenic Republic Ministry of Culture

ISBN 0-572-02217-4

Printed in Great Britain by St Edmundsbury Press, Bury St Edmunds, Suffolk

DEDICATION

To Kate, for her perseverance, support and constant belief

CONTENTS

FOREWORD

After we published our first book we were surprised and delighted to receive a sustained influx of letters from all around the world. It seemed that people of all kinds wanted to share interesting facts with us and quite a number of these new contacts led to an ongoing exchange of ideas.

The letter that arrived from Alan Butler was definitely interesting and was placed on the pile for a prompt reply. Unfortunately, due to a combination of work pressures and chaotic filing, it was actually many months before we made contact with Alan, but when we did speak it became clear that there was a great deal of common ground between us. We arranged to meet Alan and his wife Kate in a quiet Yorkshire pub to hear in more detail about Alan's researches over the past few years.

It was an enjoyable encounter. The beer was good and the conversation quite amazing. After a short time Alan reached into his pocket and placed a small, flat clay object on the table in front of us and asked us to inspect it. It was far from impressive: a scratched spiral on both sides and some meaningless pictograms dotted within them. He told us it was a faithful copy of the 4,000-year-old Minoan 'Phaistos Disc'.

It looked like some New Age talisman or perhaps a prop for a second-rate seaside fortune-teller. But the story Alan told us was far stranger than we could ever have imagined. He called it a 'Bronze Age computer disc', which sounded rather fanciful, but as we listened we could not help but be impressed by Alan's detailed knowledge of ancient history and his solid grasp of mathematics.

As we left Alan and Kate that evening we reflected on what we had heard and concluded that it was too well reasoned to reject out of hand, but it was too controversial a theory to accept without careful testing. What Alan had told us was that this little lump of baked clay conclusively demonstrated that Bronze Age peoples had possessed a super-elegant measurement system that made our modern metric systems seem hopelessly limited and clumsy.

According to Alan, the Disc measured the passage of days with a fantastic degree of accuracy and more importantly it revealed an underlying system of maths that could even measure the circumference of the Earth to within a few hundred metres.

In due course, Alan sent us his manuscript and we set to work at once, checking for errors in his calculations or flaws in his reasoning.

Alan's mathematics proved to be impeccable. Everything that was checkable was found to be correct and the evidence supported his analysis. But we were still not ready to be convinced.

We decided to ignore Alan's findings for a time and examine the Phaistos Disc to try and find an alternative explanation. After days of experimentation, we did manage to find another possible pattern. It appeared that we could argue that the Disc was actually a calendar based on a 365.25-day year, starting with the winter solstice, and that it predicted the spring and autumn equinoxes.

Now we thought we had two possible solutions and it was time to compare our results with Alan's. We needed to test which was the most likely or perhaps even to conclude that both were illusions, created by our mutual desire to solve the puzzle of the Disc.

The cold-blooded result of our test was clear. Alan had to be right. The sheer volume of supporting evidence from megalithic sources made his explanation incontrovertible.

We had to accept that the Bronze Age peoples were not only smarter than we had thought, they were also smarter than us when it came to a measuring system that fitted every aspect of the world around us and the heavens above us.

This is not just the story of one man's quest to solve an obscure and ancient riddle. It is an account of how Alan Butler rediscovered a prehistoric system of maths that was lost to the world even before Moses led the Israelites to the promised land.

Read, enjoy and prepare to be humbled by the pure skill of our distant ancestors.

Christopher Knight and Robert Lomas
Authors of *The Hiram Key* and *The Second Messiah*

INTRODUCTION

The Phaistos Disc is largely unknown outside Crete. It occupies a place in a small museum on the island. To look at, the Disc is not as awe-inspiring as the great pyramids of Egypt or as evocative as the stone circle at Stonehenge. The Phaistos Disc will never have thousands of people standing in front of it in breathless wonder, as do the treasures of the boy-king Tutankhamen or the terracotta army of China. Yet the Phaistos Disc is of great historical importance.

The thought of gleaming gold and precious jewels, sleeping for centuries beneath burial mounds or under the debris of great, fallen cities, has inspired people to travel the world, pick in hand, in the hope of finding some glistening hoard. Today, archaeologists tell you that the discovery of such precious items is incidental and that it is not the reason for their life-long dedication to the science. The painstaking business of removing the grime from the remains of the daily events of life from long ago is the object of the modern archaeologist. A broken comb, part of a preserved shoe or even the remnants of a midden may have much more to say about a long-dead society than the fantastic jewels that bedecked its kings and princesses.

The true worth of a historical artefact may not even be evident at the time of its discovery and the most precious item of all may only present itself slowly, so that, like carefully unwrapping the blackened and dusty bandages of a mummy, it takes long, patient hours before the treasure meets the light of day. Similarly, the understanding of a particular find may take long months of painstaking investigation. It may take decades.

So it has been with this small clay disc from Phaistos, which has been pondered over for 90 years or more. I have endeavoured to look at this fascinating object with a fresh perspective. For the first time in 4,000 years, something of the truth underlying the Disc can now be revealed. This is the story of the detective work that led me to discover the true nature of the Phaistos Disc. This, in turn, has brought me to a very different way of looking at our distant ancestors, not in terms of what they could produce in material wealth but rather in terms of the knowledge that they acquired and carefully handed on from generation to generation.

It has long been suspected that in the late Stone Age and early Bronze Age there was a growing desire to make sense of the changing patterns that the peoples of those times witnessed in the heavens. I believe that the Phaistos Disc is the proof, not only of what these people were looking for but also of what they actually discovered. It shows the formula upon which Stonehenge and probably many of the other megalithic monuments were built. It indicates the accuracy of a calendar that would not be bettered until the Middle Ages. The Phaistos Disc proves that Bronze Age cultures were able to handle mathematics of a sophisticated degree and it implies that there was a great traffic in knowledge across the vastness of Europe.

The Phaistos Disc may even suggest that the very basis of all our scientific knowledge stems from this long-dead civilisation.

The routes I have followed in order to reach various conclusions involve some fairly complex mathematics. If readers wish to bypass the workings and move straight to the conclusions, that's fine. If you don't want to work through the detailed mathematical explanations, simply skip over the text which is presented between dotted rules.

CHAPTER ONE

THE QUEST
BEGINS

There could surely be no more appropriate place on Earth to start a quest than Crete. The island's stark, white mountains thrust their peaks into the azure blue of the cloudless sky, towering thousands of feet above lush plains that have for countless centuries made Crete a Garden of Eden. Sometimes on a warm summer evening, clouds roll in from the sea, and across the ghostly mountain peaks the sky god fires off thunderbolts created, it was once said, far below these same mountains in a subterranean forge by Haphaestos, the lame smith of the gods. The awesome power of Haphaestos's thunderbolts rip the air asunder and the very gates of Hades seem to be thrown open. Rain falls in torrents and rivers of mud carry the rich silt to the plains below. Then, as suddenly as it started, the storm is over. After a few moments, one brave cicada begins to chirp, then dozens more join in. The fragrance of evening gradually returns. Only a low rumble in the far distance indicates that Hera is using her wiles to soothe her temperamental husband, placating his sudden fury as only a goddess can.

This is the Crete that the Minoans knew. Gnarled, old olive trees still grow here as they did 4,000 years ago. Olive oil was once stored at Knossos in the huge vessels which can still be seen today at the site of the ancient palace, now empty and unused in thousands of years. Even today, it is possible to walk all day on the tortured and twisting donkey tracks – some of which are described on the map as 'roads' – without meeting another soul. It easy to believe that the island's first goddess never left these quiet places; maybe as you walk in some remote field your footsteps are the first

13

The start of my quest: a small clay tablet in a museum on a holiday island.

to touch this ancient soil since the Olympian gods forsook this spot in favour of the darker and more foreboding mountains of the mainland. But even those great masters of mankind's destiny sprang from the womb of the first goddess here on Crete. Crete was the birthplace of the gods.

Far below the mountain, where the great sky god Zeus is said to have been born, is the modern town of Malia where my wife and I were staying during a holiday on Crete. Among its shops and markets with their gaudy tourist bric-a-brac, I first saw the Phaistos Disc or at least a facsimile of it. About 15 centimetres (6 inches) in diameter, it stood in a shop window. Made of baked red clay, it was incised with a spiral design. Spirals such as this have been captivating my imagination ever since I was a child, for there are examples of them to be found almost everywhere in Western Europe. Indeed, my earliest interest in Stone Age and Bronze Age cultures had been fired by my seeing designs such as these carved

14

The reverse side of the Disc shows a different
pattern of images and symbols.

on to rocks on the moors above Ilkley in my native Yorkshire in
northern England.

The design on the Disc consisted of an incised spiral with
another spiral of symbols or pictograms within it and a series of
broken radial lines cutting the sequence of pictograms into
phrases. Each of the pictograms must have been carved into a stone
which was then pressed into the soft clay prior to baking the Disc.
The spiral line and the radial lines seemed to have been added after
the symbols since in places they appeared to make slight detours to
make allowances for the pictograms. The pictograms were
mysterious. They bore a resemblance to Egyptian writing but they
also had something about them of the New World. Gazing at the
white marks etched into the deep red of the clay, I was struck by
the feeling that I had seen this object before or something that
looked very like it. I intuitively felt that I was looking at a calendar.
The symbols were in groups within the radial lines and there were

clearly 30 major groups or divisions which could be significant in terms of a calendar. The Disc also reminded me a little of a plaque that had been found in Central America; this had subsequently turned out to be a sophisticated calendar of the Mayan culture. Was the Phaistos Disc a calendar?

I next saw the Phaistos Disc a couple of days later when my wife and I visited the Minoan palace at Knossos. The sheer size of the ruins at Knossos offer a clue to the importance of the Minoan civilisation that flourished on Crete up until about 1450 BC. The Minoans were builders in a grand manner and, though it is always difficult to judge the genuine scale of a building when only the foundations and a few supporting walls survive, the palace appeared to go on for ever. I later came to know what Knossos must have looked like in its prime but the importance of my first visit to the site was that I was able to purchase a large picture of the Phaistos Disc from the official souvenir shop at the entrance. Armed with this, I returned to my hotel for an evening by the pool and the chance to study the artefact in greater detail – or at least a picture of it.

George, who owned part of the hotel where we were staying, was a jovial soul who appeared to have a cousin occupied in every mercantile and service trade practised in Crete. As with so many Cretans, George went far beyond common courtesy in the friendship he extended to us and as soon as he saw the photograph I had bought at Knossos he wanted to tell me all he knew of the Phaistos Disc. This was my introduction to a mystery that had stumped archaeologists for decades: no one knew what the Disc was or for what purpose it had been made. It was an enigma.

It had been found around the turn of the century, not at Knossos but in another Minoan palace at Phaistos. George told me that he was suspicious of the circumstances surrounding its discovery and he informed me that he was of the opinion that there may have been more than one disc found at Phaistos. He thought that the others had been taken off the island; he believed that what had become known as the Phaistos Disc was the only one to remain in Crete. He asked me if I had a photograph of the other side of the disc and was surprised when I admitted that I did not even know that it was double-sided.

Early the next day when we were having breakfast, George

turned up at the table. He had been working until 3 a.m. to my certain knowledge but appeared to be as bright as a button. He handed me a package. Intrigued, I opened it and to my delight discovered that it contained a replica of the Phaistos Disc. It was exactly the same as the one I had seen in the shop the previous day. That settled it. The rest of our holiday was spent chasing up literature and information relating to the Disc or in trying to make some sense of the lines and symbols covering both sides of the strange disc of red clay. By the time we flew out of Crete at the end of our holiday, I knew enough to conjecture that there was much more to the Phaistos Disc than anyone had so far realised. And I had already decided that somehow we would have to come back again to Crete and very soon so that I could pursue the secret of the Phaistos Disc.

On examining the copy of the Disc, I was intrigued to find that the reverse side had not 30 but 31 major divisions. The ratio of pictograms to radial lines was more or less the same, however; there were 123 pictograms contained within the 31 lines – I decided to call this side A – and there were 119 pictograms within 30 lines on side B. What this might mean I had no way of knowing, though there seemed to be the germ of a mathematical relationship in the pictograms and lines that was worth pursuing. Perhaps the Disc displayed two months from a 12-month calendar. If so, the pictograms might conceivably spell out the names of the days; and it seemed possible that the Minoan year might have contained a similarly convoluted system of months to our own.

What information regarding the Disc I had not been able to find in an English translation in Crete, I now began to put together from specialist bookshops and libraries all over England. Unfortunately, it amounted to very little. The same sort of ideas were coming up time and again. The pictograms looked vaguely like Egyptian hieroglyphics and since it was known that Minoan Crete had made contacts with the civilisation on the Nile, it was generally assumed that there must be some connection between Egyptian hieroglyphics and the pictograms on the Phaistos Disc. Unfortunately, since nobody could be certain of the language spoken by the Minoans, it was very unlikely that the pictograms would ever be deciphered. It was not even known whether the pictograms were part of a phonetic alphabet or if they were ideograms; in other words, whether each picture represented a sound or syllable within a word so that several of them went to make up a word, or if each one was an ideogram that stood for a separate idea or concept like house, man, field. Most authorities chose to stay firmly on the fence. Some even went so far as to assert that some of the symbols were phonetic while a few of them may have ideogram components.

Explanations varied wildly about what the Disc said – hardly surprising since no one had deciphered it. One expert claimed it was a ritual prayer or chant. This was based on the fact that some of the groups of pictograms, especially on side A of the Disc, were repeated at various intervals, indicating the name of some deity whose power and influence was being sought in the prayer. Another academic proclaimed that the Disc contained a series of instructions from a Minoan king, detailing the work necessary for building a new palace. It was even suggested by some that the Disc was not of Minoan origin at all and that it may have been brought to Crete from somewhere else. This idea has now fallen out of favour since numerous other examples of the type of pictogram on the Phaistos Disc have been found in Crete, indicating that the Disc was almost certainly of local manufacture.

I was not especially impressed with any of these suggestions. For one thing, the way the pictograms were distributed between the two sides of the Disc led me to believe that if these were indeed words, a different language or dialect seemed to have been used on side A from that incised on side B. But all my attempts to make sense of the pictograms only brought me frustration. I was getting nowhere.

The first breakthrough came when I stopped thinking about the pictograms in terms of what they might *say* and started to look at them in terms of their *numbers* on each side. I was amazed at what I discovered. Numbers appeared to be the key, not words. This was of far-reaching significance and extremely exciting. In time, I came to understand the Minoans' obsession with numbers; for now, I was beginning to learn a great deal about this fascinating and apparently unique culture.

CHAPTER TWO

THE MINOANS

The history of the Minoan civilisation is rather sketchy. Archaeological evidence suggests that the first settlers probably arrived on Crete before 3000 BC and came from what is now Turkey. Around 2800 BC, communities began to form and what we now call the Minoan civilisation probably started around 2600 BC when neolithic life gave way to a more ordered existence. The first palaces were being built by 2000 BC but these were small in comparison to the magnificent structures that came later.

Crete has always been subject to earthquakes and successive quakes inevitably took their toll of the palaces. When a palace was destroyed by an earthquake, it was rebuilt on a grander scale. Knossos in the north of the island, Malia 20 miles to the east, and Phaistos in the south are chief among the ruins of these great palaces. These once had beautiful murals on the walls and contained extensive treasuries, storehouses built on a massive scale, and all the luxuries of life. Such palaces became centres of excellence and small cities grew up round their walls. Trade flourished. Crete is blessed with many natural harbours and the seafaring Minoans traded with Greece, the northern Mediterranean and Egypt.

Nothing much is known about the system of government in Crete during the Minoan period. However, a high degree of cooperation is evident in Minoan society; the palaces were barely fortified, suggesting a peaceful way of life. Aspects of martial pursuits and warfare are almost totally lacking in Minoan art. Mythology relates that the Minoans had an impressive navy to secure their shores and to combat piracy but, although Minoan outposts are known to have existed all round the shores of the Mediterranean, there is no indication that these people were ever conquerors. Yet the Greeks later told lurid tales about King Minos (after whom the civilisation is named), claiming he ruled the Mediterranean with an iron fist, suggesting a more war-like society than the unfortified palaces and an absence of martial subjects in Minoan art would imply.

The Minoans left little to tell us who they were and how they lived and we know nothing of their language. No statue or portrait of a Minoan king has ever been found on Crete. We know that the Minoans became accomplished craftsmen and that they were especially fond of loops and spirals like many Stone Age and Bronze Age peoples all over Western Europe. I have always considered that the almost universal obsession with this motif in early art is religious in origin. Decorative frescos adorned the walls of the richly ornamented palaces, carved seals have been found in their hundreds and the Minoans were especially fond of the sumptuously decorated pottery which has been found in abundance. Workers in pottery, stone, ivory and gold seem to have been employed within walls of the palaces that were not merely secular in nature but which must have been considered to be hallowed ground in their own right.

The Minoans shunned the ostentatious temples of the Nile and later Greece in favour of revered caves up in the mountains, as well as small crypts within the palaces which may have been man-made replicas of the caves. The sky god, the forerunner of Zeus whom the Greeks attested was born on Crete, was worshipped among the peaks where the flaming forks of his powerful wrath could be observed on any stormy summer night. The goddess of nature could be found in forest clearings and with her consort on any mountain peak. There are many examples of seals and pottery bearing representations of devotees inside the palaces, as well as out in the wild places of the island. Representations that could be said to symbolise the gods and goddesses are a little difficult to validate. Especially in the case of the goddess of nature, it is often impossible to determine whether the figures are priestesses or even queens, rather than deities. Examples of worshippers before male forms are quite rare. This has led some historians to conclude

An eggshell cup discovered in the Tamare Cave
on Crete, once a place of worship.

that the religion of the Minoans was geared exclusively towards feminine deities, though representations of the sky god and of the bull games that regularly took place on the island would seem to show that the powers of nature and fertility also had masculine aspects to their characteristics.

Miniature shrines have been found but these are usually devoid of decoration apart from doves adorning the tops of pillars, the dove frequently being represented in a holy manner. The full-size shrines existed beneath the palaces. Depressions round the bases of pillars within the low shrines show that libations of oil were poured directly on to the pillars. But where were the images of their gods? It seemed that the Minoans had no need of images in order for them to worship. If the Minoans believed that the gods resided in nature, then perhaps they also believed that they could hardly be modelled in clay or stone. The Minoans were a nature-loving people and they might have believed that the gods were around them all the time, up in the mountains, among the fertile plains, in the olive groves and in the running water.

However, because of what I felt the Phaistos Disc represented, I was beginning to suspect that the Minoans might have worshipped something else besides nature. If the Disc was indeed a calendar, it was reasonable to assume that the Minoans studied the heavens. We have already seen evidence that more than suggests that they did. Did the Minoans also worship the heavenly bodies that they observed moving across the sky at regular intervals? This was an exciting possibility. The manifestation of these heavenly bodies to the Minoans could have persuaded them that earthly representations were out of the question – hence no statues. For this to make sense, the Minoans would have had to have believed that the gods were born in the mountain caves before taking to the heavens. It was an intriguing possibility but I needed evidence to support the idea. As I delved deeper and formulated my ideas about the Phaistos Disc, I began to realise that the evidence I needed was there right in front of me on the Disc itself. And I kept coming back to the numbers. Numbers were very definitely important.

Four major Minoan palaces (Malia, Knossos, Phaistos and Zakro) have been discovered and excavated on Crete, in addition to dozens of smaller mansions, settlements, ports and religious sites. The population of the island during these remote times was probably quite high. The palaces certainly did not stand in lonely isolation, for it is known that sizeable settlements crowded round their gates. Much of our present knowledge of Minoan history comes to us courtesy of Sir Arthur Evans who excavated extensively on Crete in the early part of this century. Although some of the speculative reconstruction undertaken by Evans at Knossos has been the subject of considerable criticism in more recent times, he was in the main a conscientious and skilled archaeologist who endeavoured to carefully unwrap the shrouds of time that had been wound round the Minoan era.

The present-day visitor to Knossos, which was undoubtedly the most magnificent of all the palaces, is faced with an archaeological site of such proportions that it is absolutely vital to employ a guide or to have some idea of the layout of the palace in advance. It is within this palace that the labyrinth is supposed to have existed with the Minotaur living at its centre. Fanciful this tale may be, except for two facts. The word labyrinth is derived from the ancient word 'labrys', meaning double axe. This is a motif encountered time and again on Crete and it is suggested that Knossos may have been known as the Palace of the Double Axes. In addition, the ground plan of the palace is complex. With its many connecting passages, rooms and light wells, Theseus could be forgiven for believing that here was a maze of epic proportions.

Each of the Minoan palaces was built round a long central court. The buildings are orientated so that the court runs slightly off the north–south axis. In the case of Knossos, stone-clad façades with tapering pillars and fine doorways once faced on to the central court from all sides. The building may have been four or even five floors in height in parts and must have formed an impressive structure, rising from the natural mound that was shaved and contoured for its construction. The later palace at Knossos was built exclusively in stone, though supporting pillars were made from tree trunks. The pillars tapered downward and were not usually fluted. Vast staircases were also supported by pillars and feats of engineering were undertaken at which architects have marvelled for decades. Where rooms lacked windows of their own, light wells were provided to supply light from above. Rooms were airy and well ventilated with long removable screens both to reduce the size of some rooms and to regulate the temperature inside the building.

The whole palace at Knossos is provided with a drainage system of an excellence probably not seen again until Roman times. In the so-called Queen's Apartments there is a bathroom and a toilet that utilised a modern-style wooden seat and also, remarkable for the period, a flushing cistern. The building was vast. True, there were strongholds and palaces elsewhere in the world being built at the same time as Knossos that could rival this remarkable palace for ground area but few had the fine quality the Minoans achieved.

To construct the palace of Knossos in the first place, vast quantities of earth had to be removed from the top of the mound which may already have had a ritual significance for it had been inhabited for centuries prior to Minoan times. Much space in the palace was given over to storage areas. There is evidence of olive-pressing and wine-making, and huge jars still to be found on the site bear testimony to the large quantities of honey, grain and olive oil that were stored. It has been estimated that many hundreds of people probably lived within the palace; many of them were probably court officials, artisans and servants. All of these people would have been fed from the palace food stores. The impression is of a flourishing, affluent society, producing more food than

What remains of the courtyard at the palace at Knossos.

it needed and exporting the residue.

The ritual rooms were in the western wing of the rectangle, together with the storerooms. Staterooms formed much of the eastern wing and these may well have overlooked gardens and formally landscaped areas. Many of the narrow corridors still to be found in some parts of the building attest to the labyrinthine feel of such a large and solid structure, though in the formal apartments and larger connecting corridors, light streamed in to fall on wonderful frescos. These depicted every possible facet of human life on the island, as well as showing marine creatures such as dolphins at play (see page 118). Naturalistic scenes are much in evidence throughout the whole of Minoan art. Everywhere was a riot of vivid colour.

The pillars and colonnades on all sides of the palace were probably red, as was the plaster that filled the cracks between the stone slabs on the floor. Chequered patterns of various colours were used extensively and frescos depicting parts of the palace in its prime show just how fond of ornamentation the people of Crete actually were. Flat roofs were often lined with sacred horns in stone

*Some of the huge storage vessels still remain
for modern visitors to admire.*

or plaster (see page 165). These decorations formed a sort of castellation round the palace. With the knowledge that the Minoan priests and priestesses appear to have had of the Sun's journey through the summer and winter sky, it seems likely that the sacred horns were actually used as sighting brackets for winter, summer and equinox solar positions, especially when the orientation of the palace is borne in mind.

Inspecting the endless rooms and the expertly laid drainage, and taking into consideration that there had once been access to running water, and contemplating the general scale of the palace at Knossos, together with the equally splendid example at Phaistos and the slightly more 'regional' example at Malia, one could hardly fail to marvel at the accomplishments of the master craftsmen who had toiled to build such lasting monuments to Bronze Age accomplishment. In the case of the wonderfully supported staircases, the Minoans must have had a remarkable knowledge of stresses and forces to have been able to construct them. Smaller buildings surrounded the palaces. These are of equal architectural worth, as are the many villas and townships dotted round the island. Ordinary dwelling houses were often built on two or three levels, many with penthouses on the roof which would have allowed the inhabitants to sleep out in the warm breeze on the hottest summer nights.

Outside the towns, there is good evidence to believe that a network of roads connected the centres of commerce, religion and habitation. These, too, seem to have been carefully maintained so that wooden carts with wide wheels, and subsequently chariots, could trundle along them back and forth to the ports, fetching and carrying gold for the smith, rich cloth from North Africa, pigments for dyeing and paint, metal ingots for tools and weapons, and ivory and precious minerals. In return, the same carts may have left the palaces loaded down with what was undoubtedly the finest pottery available at the time. There were cups as thin as eggshells, jars and votive vessels alive with life and colour. Woollen fleeces, honey, perhaps grain and certainly olive oil were all bound for the safe, rocky anchorages; gifts for the Pharaohs of Egypt or necessities for the small Minoan settlements springing up on the shores beyond the northern and western horizons.

Aside from the skill necessary to erect buildings such as those at Knossos and Phaistos, one can perceive the existence of a complex infrastructure in a society that moved goods about on the scale achieved by the rulers of Crete. This is reminiscent of the ordered and generally serene world of the Incas in pre-Columbian America, though infinitely more fluid and somehow more alive. There must have been a bureaucracy and it surely filtered down through all strata of society. Strict taxes in kind must have been levied, while a required amount of work for the state machine may also have been part of the price of the *Pax Minoica* which endured for centuries.

We could hypothesise a pyramidal system with a king or possibly a queen at its apex and which in later years was probably based at Knossos. Control may have been exercised sideways via palace officials and then on down the line to local governors residing in villas and maybe the smaller palaces elsewhere on the island. Governors would be lords of their own smaller domains, exacting tribute in kind from merchants, farmers and fishermen,

*Stunning jewellery has been discovered from
the Minoan civilisation, like this bee pendant
found at Malia.*

which would be passed back up the line to fill the storerooms of
the palaces. With little indication of civil unrest during the period,
it is possible that the ration expected by the ruler was not
prohibitive, for even the likelihood of civil unrest on a large scale
would have necessitated more fortification than seems to have
been provided at Knossos and its sister palaces.

It is even suggested that a degree of individual enterprise
could have entered into the scenario. There are certainly villas
close to some of the ports and these residences may have belonged
to rich merchants who traded in their own right. What allegiance
such individuals would have had to the autocracy is not clear,
though absolute independence in such a situation must surely have
led on occasion to rivalry and eventual civil strife, for which again
there is no real evidence. There is a feeling of a society generally at
ease with itself and perhaps one in which the embryo of the later
democratic ideals of Greece may have been quietly growing. This,
of course, could all be mere fanciful conjecture, though the
Minoans were clearly a free-spirited people and may have taken no
more kindly to autocratic subjugation than do the modern
inhabitants of Crete today, whose adage is still voiced all over the
island, 'Better dead than a slave'.

*Known as the 'Blue Ladies' fresco at Knossos,
this clearly shows the elaborate hairstyles
favoured by the wealthy.*

The Minoans seem to have had a strong sense of their own identity. Personal adornment, especially female adornment, was ostentatious. Men were always portrayed wearing little more than a loin-cloth, whereas the queens or priestesses sported long, full skirts with flounces of material, somewhat reminiscent of the dresses worn by Spanish flamenco dancers. Tight-waisted jackets enhanced the feminine aspect of the figure and pushed the bared breasts upward and inward. Headbands or large hats were favoured and fashions came and went, judging by the surviving pictures and statuary, at least within the female section of the ruling classes.

An understanding of ancient history is built upon a mixture of evidence and conjecture and, in the case of the Minoans who appear to have left little written evidence behind them (none of which has so far been deciphered in any case), there are inevitably large gaps in our knowledge which can only be filled by intelligent guesswork. However, what cannot speak cannot lie and the thick stone walls of Knossos, spread across so many acres at the top of their mound close to modern Heraklion, are testimony to a people who were accomplished and confident, not only in their own world but as individuals who could proudly hold up their heads in the halls of the divine Pharaohs of Egypt. This was a people to be reckoned with, as wall paintings and grave goods found in Egypt which show the kingdom's connections with Crete seem to testify. In the end, however, it may turn out that what they gave the world in terms of acquired knowledge was far more important than the most precious artefact ever to leave the workshops of Knossos.

CHAPTER THREE

THE PHAISTOS DISC

The Minoan language is unknown to us. It was probably a pre-Hellenic tongue, though it was almost certainly not the same language spoken by the Mycenaeans who established themselves on Crete after about 1450 BC; fragments of Mycenaean writing have been deciphered while Minoan writing has not. Inscriptions left on Crete by the Mycenaean rulers are in an early form of Greek script and are now more or less fully understood. Even as late as 100 BC, there were small communities in isolated parts of Crete who still spoke a language that was alien to visitors from the mainland and even to most inhabitants of the island. This language was most probably related to the Minoan tongue.

If the symbols on the Phaistos Disc are indeed a written language, it is necessary to establish what form of writing it is before any sort of translation can be made of them. Much early writing was idiomatic, with each symbol representing an idea or concept. Quite complex messages could be conveyed with this form of writing but it is difficult to decipher without knowing what some of the symbols represent before attempting to translate the whole message. For example, a pictogram of a man walking followed by another of an ear of wheat might mean that the individual is going out to work in the fields, though the ear of wheat could just as easily represent a place, perhaps a particular town or village. Thus the message may indicate that the individual is going to Malia, for example. On the other hand, the symbols might not represent an individual going somewhere but something else quite different. The possibilities are virtually endless and unless

A simplified representation of side A of the Phaistos Disc.

some artefact is found containing the same symbols set against the same message in a known script, the difficulties of deciphering the symbols are very considerable indeed. It was the finding of the Rosetta stone, which contained information presented in three different writing systems, that proved to be the decisive step in translating Egyptian hieroglyphics.

The Minoan symbols could, on the other hand, represent some form of phonetic system in which the symbols represent simple sounds that can be strung together to make words. However, the symbols would not form an alphabet in the modern sense. If the symbols do indeed represent sounds, this could explain why so many of them were available to the makers of the Disc. Another option is that the symbols on the Disc are a combination of

A simplified representation of side B
of the Phaistos Disc.

idiomatic and phonetic components. Many authorities now consider this to be the case. If this turns out to be so, the difficulties of translating the Phaistos Disc are still considerable. We may never know what the message is – if indeed it is a message in the form of words making up sentences.

In the years since the Phaistos Disc was found, many people have devoted themselves tirelessly to the task of interpreting the symbols. There is still no interpretation that has gained general acceptance. Advocates of the Disc being written in a language foreign to Minoan Crete, perhaps from the north coast of Africa or the region that is now Turkey, have made some impressive attempts at an interpretation. However, the fact that other artefacts exist in Crete with pictograms very similar to those used on the Phaistos

Disc lessens the chance of them being imported from outside. Most experts now doubt the importation theory and believe the symbols to be native to Minoan Crete. If they are correct and the import theory is false, translations made from these archaic languages must be suspect; but they may be entirely wrong.

A ritual hymn or prayer has been suggested as the most likely subject of the writing on the Disc. The reason that this is the most favoured explanation at present rests mainly on the fact that some of the phrases are repeated, especially on side A of the Disc. The explanation put forward by the advocates of this theory is that within the repeating phrases we should see the name of a particular deity being repeated, as with chants in invocations from other parts of the world. But this is supposition because no one knows what the writing on the Disc means.

It seemed to me that it was time to look at the Disc in a different way and to concentrate on the puzzles that linguists had failed to address. This was where the numbers started to come in and in a most remarkable way.

One of the first things that I noticed when comparing side A with side B of the Disc is just how different the two faces really are in terms of composition. Most of the repeated phrases are on side A (in this context, a 'phrase' is a series of pictograms between two of the radial lines). There is something very odd about the spacing between these repeated phrases, even if this is a ritual hymn. Now, this spacing could just be a coincidence, or it could be a clear indication of a mathematical relationship between the phrases on side A. Whenever a phrase is repeated, its subsequent appearance in the spiral is always located a specific number of phrases after its first appearance and that number is always divisible by three. For example, the very first phrase, Phrase 1, which comprises a flower, a bald man's head and an oar, is repeated in Phrase 4 which is three phrases after its first appearance. Similarly, Phrase 3, which is a complex collection of objects that include plants, a comb-like object or agricultural implement, and a warrior's head and a shield, can be found again in Phrase 15 which is 12 phrases after its first appearance. Many phrases are duplicated in this way but there is one phrase that is repeated on the Disc not twice but three times. This first appears in Phrase 10 and contains a horn, a dove, a shield and the warrior's head. It is repeated in Phrase 13 (three phrases away) and again at Phrase 16 (six phrases away).

There are many instances of repeated phrases on side A of the Disc and they all follow the same mathematical rule; there is not a single deviation from this pattern. It would seem highly unlikely that this is attributable to chance. It must have been deliberate. And if it was deliberate, it is highly probable that it was meant to signify something.

Side B of the Disc is subtly different in terms of content, the length of the phrases, the pictograms used, and the way that the phrases are repeated. There are too many differences between the two faces of the Disc to itemise them all here but one of the most important relates to the number of symbols that comprise each phrase, i.e. the number of symbols bracketed between any two of the radial lines that intersect the spiral. On side A of the Disc, they vary between two and seven, while on side B there are never more than five symbols to a phrase. Certain symbols that appear regularly on side A only appear once or twice on side B. Similarly, certain symbols that appear on side B appear only once or twice on side A. There are fewer repeated phrases on side B and there appears to be no mathematical relationship between the repeated phrases. But on each face of the Disc, there is a mathematical relationship between the number of symbols and the number of dividing lines. Side A contains 123 symbols within 31 lines; side B has 119 symbols within 30 lines. In each case, the ratio of symbols to lines is 3.96:1 (roughly four symbols to every line).

As far as I am aware, nobody has ever suggested that the Phaistos Disc may have a mathematical meaning in addition to – or, indeed, instead of – a linguistic one. This is not to suggest that I am against the idea of the symbols carrying a linguistic message in addition to a mathematical one. In fact, I am certain that they do – we just do not know what it is yet. It seemed to me that the symbols had been deliberately manipulated so that they carried some sort of linguistic message but in a way that also allowed them to function as markers within a mathematical framework. The Minoans must have created this multipurpose message for a specific reason. For the Disc to contain mathematical information, the Minoans must have intended the Disc to be used as a tool for some purpose – a 'calculating machine' of some sort, perhaps.

The idea that the Phaistos Disc might have been a sort of

calculating machine that conveyed a linguistic message as well is not as far-fetched as it might appear at first sight. After all, it is quite easy to create such a disc using modern language. What is more, the message could take the form of a prayer or chant and yet still contain, for the initiated, the mathematical basis on which the 'machine' works. To demonstrate this I have invented an example of this sort of message. The example below is set out in a linear fashion for the sake of simplicity but it could just as easily be set in a spiral round a disc like the pictograms on the Phaistos Disc.

Side A of the hypothetical disc could read:

To | the | praise | and | glory | of | the | Great | Goddess | who | orders | the | planets | in | their | path | and | who | carries | the | Young | God | from | birth | to | death | and | on | to | birth | again |

On side B, the words could read:

The | Bull | carries | the | Great | God | across | the | sky | sacred | in | the | caves | and | the | hill | shrine | Praise | be | to | the | double | axe | the | symbol | of | the | Great | God's | power |

I stress that these examples are not intended to be taken as possible interpretations of the symbols on the Phaistos Disc. However, they do comprise what could be seen as ritual hymns and they contain the correct number of symbols, in this case letters that make words, and the correct number of dividing lines, although I have not incorporated the Phaistos Disc repeats. As with the Phaistos Disc, the mathematical capabilities of a disc inscribed in this way would only be significant to those individuals who had been primed as to its purpose. Everyone else would only be aware of the message contained in the words. The chants themselves can be read by anyone who is literate and who understands the language in which they are written, while only the initiated could detect anything more in them.

The use of symbols rather than letters carries its own advantage, irrespective of whether the symbols are ideograms or part of a phonetic alphabet. Whatever the composition of Minoan writing may have been, it seems likely that each symbol retained an identity besides its linguistic interpretation. For example, the warrior's head which appears so often on the Phaistos Disc could represent the sky god worshipped by the Minoans, consort of the nature goddess who was very important in Minoan beliefs. With use, this symbol may have attracted a phonetic association but still be recognised for its original meaning. This being the case, the symbols could make sense when viewed one at a time or when strung together to make words. In all probability, initiates of the mathematical system viewed the symbols merely as number markers and ignored the linguistic associations. If symbol names were used rather than numbers, some confusion might have arisen when the symbols were repeated.

A later Greek tradition might also offer some clue about the intended use of the symbols. In *Works and Days*, the Greek writer Hesiod offered advice to a younger male relative about the most fortunate day of any particular period to undertake specific tasks. By the time *Works and Days* was written in the eighth century BC, each month seems to have comprised 30 days, though *Works and Days* still owes something to lunar timekeeping. Hesiod talked about a particular day of the month, for example the sixth, as being propitious for gelding goats but as boding ill for the birth or marriage of girls. Many of the tasks ascribed to particular days in *Works and Days*, which form a rigid and quite specific list, fall in line with established lunar lore. It was always considered, for example, that seeds grow better if planted at the time of the new moon. There was a sympathetic magic in this belief, since it was thought that the seed would germinate and grow with the face of the Moon. However, not all advice offered by Hesiod can be viewed as being lunar in nature and some of it was obviously geared to the actual day of a month. This means that Hesiod and his contemporaries were believers in numerology and considered that numbers had a significance of their own.

Obsessed as they seem to have been by numbers, it is likely that the Minoans also believed that specific days were auspicious for specific tasks or events and it is just possible that the Phaistos Disc symbols were intended to be used in this way. It is possible that as individual markers, and within the framework of a sacred chant, the symbols on the Disc indicated lucky associations for a particular day, the deity ruling that day, or some task considered to be propitious if undertaken on a given day.

From the outset, I endeavoured to find answers to some of the puzzles of the Phaistos Disc, answers which might lie outside a linguistic meaning. In other words, I was fascinated not so much in what the Disc might *say* but in what it could *do*. It looked as though the Disc had been intended to perform a specific function. And it was looking more and more as though the Disc was some sort of calendar.

CHAPTER FOUR

A QUESTION OF TIME

The calendar we use today might well be considered distinctly messy if viewed by an alien visitor from another world. Containing four months with 30 days, seven with 31 days and one month with 28 or 29 days depending on which year it is, it has been the subject of innumerable verses to help people work out its intricacies. We must all have struggled initially with the 'Thirty days hath September, April, June and November' aid to memory. How did we manage to arrive at such an apparently odd system in the first place?

The earliest civilisations seem to have relied almost exclusively on the Moon for their divisions of the year. It is from the word 'moon' that the word 'month' is derived and there are a little over 12 full-moon cycles in one solar year. The lunar quarters (that is from new moon to first quarter, from first quarter to full moon and so on) each take about seven days. Splitting up the Moon's cycle in this way is convenient and was the origin of the modern week. However, even this pattern is not accurate since full moon to full moon takes not 28 days but an average of 29.53 days which is not divisible by a whole number. So the lunar months do not fit neatly into the solar year and it is impossible to divide the lunar months into equal numbers of days.

The whole business starts to become complicated as soon as it is realised that the Earth takes not 365 days to complete one full revolution of the Sun but slightly less than 365.25 days. I have been looking at ancient cultures and their handling of such facts for all my adult life and even at this distance in time I can feel their frustration with the situation. A good understanding of the solar year is vital for any culture wishing to grow and harvest crops successfully. If you plant seeds too early, they will not germinate properly or they may spring up before the weather conditions are good enough to allow them to flourish. Accurate assessments of the onset of rainy seasons, dry seasons and frosts are crucial to the survival of a farming community. In fact, even before agrarian cultures began to spring up in the Middle East about 10,000 years ago it could be argued that mankind already needed to be able to measure the year with some degree of accuracy. The migrating herds followed by the hunters and gatherers of pre-agrarian cultures may not have needed a calendar in order to realise that it was the season to move on, but it would certainly have been useful for the human predators of the migrating animals to have been aware that it was time to strike camp to intercept their quarry.

In the earliest cultures, the Sun provided the information they needed. Long years of observation from special places would have told the elders of a tribe at what point on the eastern horizon the Sun could be expected to rise on the year quarters – midwinter when the Sun rises at its southernmost point, at midsummer when it reaches its northernmost point, and the spring and autumn equinoxes when it is midway between the two (the seasons are, of course, reversed in the southern hemisphere). Distant mountain peaks, an ancient tree or a boulder on the horizon would certainly have played a part in such observations, which was the reason that the 'standing place' was of such importance. In time, the sighting points became sacred places.

Where natural sighting points could not be found, man learned how to make them for himself. A village chief or wise man might sit day after day on a large termite mound, for example, to observe at what position in the eastern horizon the Sun rose each day. When the Sun was observed to reach one of its extremities, a large stick or a rock would have been placed between the observer and the point on the horizon where the solar disc had appeared. The procedure would have been repeated at the other end of the year and a third stick or boulder would have been placed between the two, representing the approximate timing of the equinoxes to indicate spring and autumn. This would have been a simple if somewhat monotonous task.

If our hypothetical tribe had moved round the countryside in

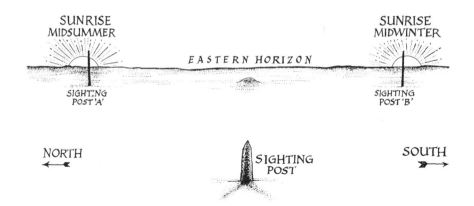

Sighting posts were used to make regular measurements of the movement of the sun across the heavens.

search of game, they would have eventually acquired several sighting points which would have been considered special places. Burials may well have taken place in their vicinity and with each successive generation the sighting points would have become more deeply revered. All that would have been really required to service the sighting points would have been to clear away vegetation that might have obscured the view, to make certain that the sighting stones or sticks had not been moved and to have kept the observation point as the most sacred place of all, because the whole business depended upon standing on a specific spot.

With agriculture came the need to be even more accurate, not only with regard to planting and harvesting but also because the whole business had probably started to take on an importance all of its own. 'OK,' reasoned the wise man or woman, 'the Sun stops travelling south when it reaches sighting post B – but what if it doesn't stop there this year? The weather will get colder and colder and eventually we will all starve to death.' Who could make the Sun turn round this year? Only the gods had such power and so it was sensible to placate them. As a result, elaborate ceremonies began to develop in order to make certain that spring and summer would return each year. These would naturally take place on the days of the sun's greatest elongation and perhaps on equinox days too.

Periodically the Moon's face would be darkened at full moon. More rarely, the solar disc itself would be eaten up and the world would be cast into unexpected darkness. The people would have been scared, wondering why it was happening. Were the gods angry? And what were the portents of this strange occurrence? Was there a pattern to such events? These were questions that must have been asked many times and it was up to the priests to supply the answers. Predictions of eclipses were the source of tremendous power, knowledge of how to make them remained in the hands of the ruling élite. It was simply a matter of calling out the whole tribe at the right time and showing them the eclipse, then promising to remove the curse or to placate the gods to allow things to return to normal once again. Few had the skills possessed by the priests and everyone could be easily convinced that ritual made the eclipse happen and could be used to make it go away again.

This was also the start of what became known as the divine mysteries; in each culture, astronomy and mathematics went hand in hand but were kept within a privileged élite. The old priests and priestesses taught the next generation, hand-picked novices who were sworn to secrecy on pain of death concerning the magic of the Sun, the Moon and planetary interactions. Only they held the right to regulate the calendars and to pass on the necessary information to the ordinary people, not the mechanism of the divine mystery but the observed results according to the heavens and the calendar. It was essential to know exactly how the days passed and the length of the solar year, as well as how to regulate the calendar accordingly. Knowledge of such mysteries, however, would have been expressly denied to anyone who was not an initiate.

As far as the modern calendar is concerned, it has been subjected to the whims and caprices of successive emperors and holy men who attempted to get the calendar working properly. All this happened many centuries ago. Our calendar is Roman in origin although it can probably be traced back as far as ancient Greece. Two emperors amended the calendar: it was altered by Julius Caesar who gave us a 31-day July and later by Augustus who gave us a 31-day August. However, the Roman calendar was not a perfect system and things began to go wrong, so that by the end of the sixteenth century the calendar days no longer came anywhere near to matching the solar days. In 1582, Pope Gregory decided enough was enough and he resolved to put matters right once and for all. Unfortunately, this meant removing ten days from the calendar in order to rectify the discrepancies that had accumulated over the centuries. Riots ensued all over Christendom as peasants complained about having ten days stolen from them. However, not all of Christendom went over to the Gregorian system; Britain stuck to the faulty Julian calendar for another 170 years. Nevertheless, even the British had to come to terms with the deficiencies of the Julian calendar and in September 1752 the Gregorian calendar was adopted. The people of Britain were no more happy about the loss of 11 days than the continental Europeans had liked losing ten days in 1582. It is the Gregorian calendar that we use today.

With the adoption of the amended calendar, things are more or less right – the calendar and the solar year are almost coincident. Of course, we have to add on an extra day every four years in order to keep the calendar straight – unless the fourth year is a century year, in which case no extra day is added, with the exception of century years that are divisible by 400 in which the extra day is added. It is all very simple and straightforward really. It works pretty well on the whole and we can all get on with our lives – even if some of us do have to work an extra day every four years without getting paid more money for the privilege.

Ancient cultures struggled to understand how the gods could have conspired to make a year 365-and-a-bit days in length, particularly if they did not understand fractions, and devised their own ways of dealing with the situation. The Egyptians opted for a 360-day year which suited their ordered minds. In reality, the Egyptians were clever enough to realise that there were more than 360 days in the year, though for several thousand years they never compensated mathematically for the extra bit of a day. The other five days were put down to festival or holiday periods which were snobbishly ignored by court mathematicians who could probably find no logical way to subdivide the year into months that made sense if these days were incorporated in their calculations. They decided that there were to be 12 months of 30 days each – which, after all, is almost the length of the period from one new moon to the next. The extra days were at the behest of gods who surely

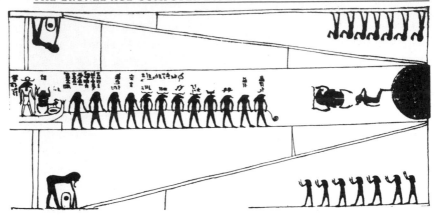

An Egyptian papyrus painting showing the sun being rolled along its course by an enormous scarab. Auf-Ra is in the boat on the left being drawn along the solar course through the underworld by the gods of the hours of the night.

could be trusted to know what they were doing. The Egyptians were perfectly happy with their system.

The Minoans, it seems, had their own way of dealing with the oddity of the solar year. The Minoans were not content to make do with a 360-day year that clearly did not match the solar year. They wanted something better, something more precise and consequently more reliable. It was a method that would give rise to early geometry, as well as teaching mankind something about mathematics.

Before we look at the Minoan year, it is essential that we take a look at how we divide the day into its component parts – 24 hours which is 1,440 minutes or 86,400 seconds. This is another hybrid system bearing no direct relationship to any outside influence. In other words, if I live in Aberdeen and you live in London and I propose to call you on the telephone at 3.10 p.m., it is important that you understand that your 3.10 p.m. is the same as mine. If our telephone conversation takes 4 minutes, the Earth will have turned about one degree of arc round its axis; if I only keep you talking for one minute, the Earth will have turned 15 minutes of arc (each degree is divided into 60 minutes). Even in our society, there is a subtle connection between these two events, though its intrinsic meaning has been lost in history. Now a minute is only understood by the majority of people as a unit of time because practically everyone on the planet has access to a clock of some sort which tells them how long a minute is. In other words, although it would be possible to look out of the window and note the position of the Sun in order to estimate the time of day, this is not directly related to the way in which we order our lives. Most of us are active during daylight hours and more or less dormant when it is dark, but this is really about as far as celestial awareness goes in our modern society.

From an astronomical point of view, it is clear that there should only be 12 hours in a day and this is undoubtedly the way that things started out. The reason for this lies in the fact that we have chosen historically to divide the ecliptic (the path that the Sun appears to take across the sky) into 12 sections known as the zodiac constellations. Since each of these constellations passes over our heads once each day, it would be logical to assume that the time taken by each zodiac constellation in its passage across the sky would be used as a means of dividing up the day. At some time in the distant past, it looks as though the 12-hour day was made into a 24-hour day in order to allow for 12 hours of daytime and another 12 hours of night-time. Measuring the passage of time has always been something of a problem, historically speaking. Shadow clocks such as sundials could be constructed to log the passage of time during the day but dealing with the passage of time at night is a rather more complicated puzzle.

The Egyptians managed to produce devices for telling the time at night, an indication of their ingenuity. However, since day and night are rarely of equal length in non-equatorial regions, the situation can become rather complicated. Once again, man's ingenuity was stretched to the full, producing a host of different ways of telling the time. Measured candles, hourglasses, water timers and a host of other inventions were all used before the invention of clocks. It was only with the invention of clockwork that it became possible to measure time accurately irrespective of whether it was light outside or dark.

My research indicated that the Minoans did their best to keep things simple and by so doing devised a system that was beautiful, as harmonious as their frescos and pottery, and surprisingly accurate. All of this is inferred from the numbers used on the Phaistos Disc. The Phaistos Disc must rank as one of the world's earliest and most remarkable calculating machines. With its help we can see how the Minoans saw the days, months and years of their lives.

CHAPTER FIVE

HOW LONG IS
A YEAR?

robably the best way to explain the evidence for Minoan astronomical practices derived from the mathematics of the Phaistos Disc is to describe the way that the culture appears to have dealt with the problem of constructing a working calendar. The investigation I have undertaken regarding the Phaistos Disc points to the fact that the Minoans, some time prior to 1700 BC, opted to celebrate a year of 366 days. This seems to have also been reflected in an embryonic system of geometry that relied on a circle of 366 degrees of arc, as opposed to the now universally accepted 360 degrees.

My reasons for considering the 366-day year as a possibility arose in part from the fact that there were 30 major divisions on one side of the disc and 31 on the other. I reasoned that if the Disc was a complete calendar in its own right and not part of a series of discs dedicated to the same year then 30 and 31 could indicate alternate months of 30 and 31 days within the same year. This being the case, and assuming that there were 12 months in the Minoan year, the duration of the year would have to be 366 days.

This is slightly longer than the tropical solar year. The tropical solar year is the time taken by the Sun to make two successive passages across the vernal equinox (the first degree of Aries which is expressed as 1° of Aries) and is about a quarter of a day longer than 365 days (365.2422 days to be exact). However, the adoption of a 366-day year does have several advantages over the 360-day year of the Egyptians or the strictly lunar-based systems adopted by other cultures that were contemporary with the Minoans. One basic problem, though, is that unless there is some way of relating the 366-day year to the solar year, any advantage gained would soon be hopelessly swamped by the inaccuracies that must ultimately accumulate. What I eventually discovered was that the method used for keeping the 366-day year in step with the solar year seemed to have been one of the primary functions of the Phaistos Disc; or at least, the primary function of the *mathematical* information contained on the Disc. Side A of the Disc has 123 symbols while side B has only 119 symbols. When these are multiplied we get 14,637. And this turns out to be only three days short of 40 years, if each year has 366 days. This was an astonishing discovery and convinced me that I was indeed dealing with a mathematical relationship.

It might be useful at this stage to explain the way that the Sun appears to move within the zodiac when viewed from the Earth as this is fundamental to an understanding of the Minoan system of counting the days. It is actually quite straightforward.

The zodiac is the backdrop of stars that appears to pass across the sky once every day. This is because of the turning of the Earth about its own axis (the axis extends through centre of the Earth and emerges at the north and south poles). The Sun, and indeed all the planets of the solar system, pass in front of this backdrop of stars. And because the constellations are so much further away from us than the Sun and the planets, a star in the constellation of Aries, for example, will always occupy the same position in the sky relative to the rest of the constellation, whereas the Sun and the planets pass from one constellation to another. Fortunately, they do this in a measurable way. The Sun takes about one month to pass through each of the 12 constellations or zodiac signs. This is the origin of the 12 months of the year. Originally, the 12 divisions of the year may well have simply been derived from the nearest whole number of lunations, the intervals between full moons. Although there are sometimes 13 full moons in an Earth year, 12 is more common. This fact may also have been partly the reason for mankind deciding upon 12 signs of the zodiac, rather than any other number.

If there were 360 days in a solar year and 360 degrees in a circle, then it follows that the Sun would travel at exactly one degree per day relative to the zodiac. Unfortunately for astronomers, this is simply not the case. Because there are 365.2422 days in the tropical solar year, the Sun travels a little less than one degree per day (0.9856 degrees per day to be exact). This is an awkward figure and makes finding the position of the Sun within the zodiac very difficult without good mathematical skills or a calculator. It also means that the Sun will not enter a particular zodiac constellation on the same day each year. This is due to the fact that there are not an exact number of days in the solar year.

The adoption of a 366-degree circle improves the situation significantly, since the number of days in the solar year (365.2422) and the number of degrees in a circle are now very nearly the same. In fact, if you have a 366-degree circle, the daily motion of the Sun is 1.002 degrees which is so close to one degree that for most practical purposes the difference is negligible – bearing in mind that the degrees of a 366-degree circle are not the same size as the degrees in a 360-degree circle; they are, of course, slightly smaller because there are more of them.

The degrees in a 366-degree circle are Minoan degrees (°M). The actual movement of 1.002° is only about seven seconds of arc (one degree is 60 minutes which is 360 seconds) away from one full degree of movement per day which would make the Sun very easy to track.

Unfortunately life is not that simple – because in reality there are not 366 days in a year. The figure of 366 is about three-quarters of a day more than the actual number of days in the solar year. Fortunately, the Minoan year of 366 days and the tropical solar year of 365.2422 days almost exactly coincide after 480 Minoan years and 481 solar years.

The number of Minoan days in 480 Minoan years is 175,680; the number of days in 481 tropical solar years is 175,681.4982. The difference is a mere 1.4982 days – roughly one and a half days.

The interesting thing about this length of time is that the number 480 is divisible by 12 which is also the number of signs in the zodiac and the number of months in a year. Twelve divides into 480 exactly 40 times. It is upon this apparent coincidence that practically all the working principles of the Phaistos Disc rely and, therefore, the Minoan understanding of the passing of time.

This is highly significant. Firstly, 480 Minoan years (which I have named the Grand Minoan Cycle) can be divided into 12 units of 40 Minoan years (I have given the name Minoan Cycle to 40

Minoan years) which is approximately 40 solar years. At these time spans, there is a definite relationship between the position of the Sun in terms of solar years and Minoan years. The difference between 40 Minoan years and 40 solar years turns out to be a little over 30 days (30.312 days to be exact). This is very close to one Minoan month which averages 30.5 days. It is very likely that the Minoan astronomers realised this and knew that by the simple expedient of removing one Minoan month from the calendar at the end of each Minoan Cycle they would find the Sun in almost exactly the same position it occupied at the start of the 40-year cycle. Since the removal of a whole month would have been a drastic expedient that would have probably played havoc with the order of things in Minoan Crete every 40 years, it is likely that the Minoans took a gentler and more acceptable approach to the problem. After all, no society can tolerate that kind of drastic upheaval on so regular a basis, and the Minoan civilisation does not appear to have suffered civil unrest.

One of the advantages of adopting a 366-day year in the first place would have been the relative ease with which nearly every astronomical computation could be made. From the Minoan point of view, there were many other advantages besides this – and we will come to these in due course, but for the time being we will stay with the advantage of easy computation. There were the daily requirements of life to be considered, including the needs of the farmers in what was an agrarian society. A 366-day year meant that there was an error of three-quarters of a day each year. The consequence of this would have been a slipping backwards of the sowing times with each passing year. If the astronomers had been unaware of this retrograde movement, this would only have been a problem when the accumulative error became so great that drastic action was necessary in order to put the calendar back on track. Such a situation arose with our own calendar in the days of Pope Gregory during the sixteenth century, when things had become so hopelessly confused that a full ten-day error had to be dealt with. However, it does not appear to have happened in Minoan Crete. The mathematics tend to show that the priests of ancient Crete knew exactly what they were doing, since there is nothing at all arbitrary about the numbers being used. If it was known that there was a one-month difference between 40 solar years and 40 Minoan years, it must also have been realised that this amounted to an error of about three days every four years. As long as an instruction was given at the right time to amend the farming calendar by three days every four years, and provided the necessary solar-based ceremonies were regulated in the same way, the 366-day year could continue indefinitely; and after 481 years it coincided with the solar calendar once again.

All the figures used so far presume that the Minoans regarded the tropical solar year to be the norm, although it is unlikely that they knew it by a name that bore any resemblance to this term. But there are other ways of measuring the year which the mathematicians of ancient Crete probably understood as well. However, no Bronze Age culture could have accurately measured the figure necessary to resolve the true value of the tropical solar year which, as we have seen, is the time between two successive passages of the Sun through the first degree of Aries. The accepted figure is 365.2422 days and is calculated to within 17 seconds of time over the whole year. Of course, nowadays we can do even better than this and arrive at a remarkably accurate figure. However, without a very accurate method of timekeeping, a figure that was correct to within 17 seconds could not have been calculated by the Minoans despite the fact that their system was quite accurate. And the Minoan system is essentially very simple. As long as the 481-year relationship between the solar year and the Minoan year was understood, the precise length of the tropical solar year was not really an issue.

My theory about the Minoans and the Phaistos Disc really began to make sense once I had come to terms with the Disc's mathematical properties. The Phaistos Disc turns out to be a machine that works on many different levels, so that, depending on which part of the Minoan system you look at, side B of the Disc can represent, for example, one month or 40 years. Presently I will explain how the Phaistos Disc, or a disc working on exactly the same mathematical principles, was used to accurately measure the Minoan Cycles. However, we must first look a little more closely at the way in which the heavens have been divided up from a historical perspective.

It is important to recognise in the first instance that the Minoans used a 12-month year, because this is fundamental to understanding the principles upon which the Phaistos Disc worked.

We have already seen that the notion of a roughly 12-month year springs from lunar observation and we have also seen that there are not 12 full moon cycles within each solar year because each cycle takes only 29.53 days to complete, so that a 12-lunation year would only take about 355 days. All the same, this is a starting point and probably one that our earliest ancestors utilised. In Spain and in other parts of the world, worked animal bones from Stone Age times have been found. Some of these carry incised marks that could well indicate a rudimentary form of lunar calendar. The Moon-based calendrical system is perpetuated to this day in some cultures; for example, the Moslem calendar is still essentially lunar. The Moon presents us with the first clue to a 12-month calendar, even though, if we are to be truly accurate, the duration of the Moon's cycles are not sufficiently long to fill the solar year exactly 12 times. If the year is to be divided accurately into 12 equal parts, some yardstick other than a lunar one is required. It seems to have been found in terms of the Sun rather than in the behaviour of his sister the Moon.

The Sun appears to make a journey through the stars during a full solar year. Of course, we now know that the Sun is essentially fixed in space (it can be considered to be fixed for our purposes although, in fact, it rotates round the centre of our galaxy, the Milky Way, along with the rest of our solar system and all the stars in the Milky Way). The Earth orbits the Sun, as do all the other planets of the solar system. However, it appears to an observer on Earth that it is the Sun and the planets that revolve round the Earth. As the Earth also completes a full turn on its own axis once every day, the whole sky can be observed to pass overhead each day. The fixed stars are, in fact, no more fixed than our Sun because they too rotate round the centre of the galaxy but they are so far away from Earth that they appear to be fixed. The distances involved are immense. The patterns that they form change very little from age to age. The Sun, Moon and all the planets of our solar system can be seen to move in a regular way across the backdrop of this vast array of stars and galaxies. Early man was aware of this essential difference between the planets and the stars. The very word 'planet' is derived from a word that means 'wanderer'.

The path taken by the Sun and the planets is not haphazard. In their journey round the Sun, as far as an Earth-based observer is concerned, all the planets stay very close to an imaginary plane extending out from the equator of the Earth into the solar system. In reality, this plane runs slightly north and south of the equator because the Earth is tilted on its axis. This tilting accounts for the seasons on Earth, since on part of her orbit, the Earth's northern hemisphere is in sunlight for longer each day, while at the opposite part of the journey round the Sun it is the southern hemisphere that benefits. During the summer, sunlight also has less atmosphere to pass through in order to warm up the hemisphere in question. Sunlight also has a greater or lesser area to illuminate, depending on the angle at which it strikes the Earth.

The plane within which the Sun and the planets travel, as seen from the Earth, is called the plane of the ecliptic and within this band of space are to be found the 12 constellations which became known as the signs of the zodiac. The constellations have strong historical significance in the mythology of mankind. In the West, nearly all the gods, goddesses, heroes and heroines of Greek mythology are to be found within these constellations. As with all the constellations, the zodiac signs are in fact quite unrelated stars at varying distances from the Earth, though they appear to form pictures that make them easy to recognise. There are 12 signs in the zodiac, spread more or less equally round the plane of the ecliptic and it takes the Sun about one-twelfth of a year to pass through one of them. The zodiac signs are a useful reference point when it comes to solar, lunar and planetary observation, for it is a certainty that each member of the solar system's family will be found somewhere within the zodiac constellations at any given point in time.

When and where the zodiac constellations were first named has always been something of a mystery. Astronomers and astrologers alike still use more or less the same reference points that have been used for thousands of years, and variations on the zodiac theme exist in all cultures of the world. However, light was shed on the origin of the zodiac by an interesting piece of research recently undertaken by two professors from Glasgow University. There is a phenomenon known as the precession of the equinoxes which occurs because the Earth 'wobbles' on its axis very much like a spinning top. The effect of this is that the point at which the plane

A representation of the zodiac constellations on the solar sphere by E. Schön, 1515.

of the ecliptic crosses the celestial equator (the celestial equator is a projection of the Earth's equator on to the sky above) does not always occur at the same part of the zodiac as would be the case if the Earth was steady in the way it turned about its own axis and did not wobble. The precession of the equinoxes is an event that takes a very long time to complete – the full cycle takes over 25,000 years. Understanding this phenomenon is a little complex and is really no more relevant to our daily lives than it was to the daily lives of the Minoans. But it does give us a clue as to when the zodiac was named.

Between 1965 and 1984, Professor Ovendon and Professor Roy of Glasgow University pondered the precession of the equinoxes and came to the conclusion that it would be possible, with the aid of a computer, to discover when and where the zodiac was first observed and recorded. The time turned out to be about 2000 BC, give or take a couple of centuries, at a place about 36 degrees from the equator. The only culture that fits these two requirements of geographical location and time is that of the Minoans on the island of Crete. No other civilisation of the time was in the right place or had sufficient knowledge to háve been able to divide up the sky in this way. Of course, it is not known by what names the Minoans knew the zodiac constellations which have changed a little even in fairly recent times but there can be little doubt that they considered there were 12 of them and that they used these as a method for measuring the plane of the ecliptic. The findings of Professors Ovenden and Roy prove that the framework of modern astronomy was laid down on the island of Crete and that it happened around the time that the Phaistos Disc was manufactured.

This was an encouraging piece of evidence, albeit indirect, not only in support of the Phaistos Disc being a calendar but also that there was a mathematical significance to the arrangement of symbols and lines on the Disc. If the Minoans had been capable of devising the zodiac, clearly they had also been capable of using this to devise a calendar. Since one-twelfth of the Sun's passage across the sky takes between 30 and 31 days, it is safe to conclude that the Minoans were aware of this and incorporated it into their calendar system. What may be more important is the fact that the Minoans clearly had the intelligence to undertake what is, after all, a fairly academic exercise, one that would only be of any use to people who were watching the planets and stars on a regular basis.

I have looked closely at the many artefacts in Heraklion Museum on Crete and, though there are many examples of hieroglyphs and linear texts, there is nothing which looks like the modern symbols by which the zodiac signs are identified. This is not really surprising. It has taken 4,000 years or more for astrologers and astronomers to arrive at the present glyphs by which the zodiac signs are known. Each culture has its own way of representing the zodiac signs and the planets, and undoubtedly the Minoan star-gazers had theirs. Some of the Minoan symbols for planets and zodiac signs may well have been included on the Phaistos Disc.

The Minoan civilisation came to an end around 1450 BC, following a great fire that destroyed many of the towns and cities. The astronomical knowledge that the civilisation had accrued was not entirely lost, however, and it was left to later Greek astronomers such as Eoduxus (409–365 BC) and Hipparchus (190–120 BC) to repeat some of the earlier observations. It is my contention that they did so without a full working knowledge of the Minoan practices and measurements and that, as a result, a corrupted version of the Minoan way of looking at the cosmos and the Earth has been passed down through the centuries.

Much of modern science stands on Greek foundations. But perhaps we are sometimes too quick to assume that all the discoveries made during the classical period by Greek men of science were in fact original discoveries and not actually *re-*discoveries of things that had been known long before the Greek civilisation was born. After all, it is known that many great Greek men of science travelled extensively in their search for knowledge. It is entirely feasible that some remnants of Minoan astronomy were preserved after the destruction of the Minoan civilisation – perhaps in Egypt, for example – and that these remnants were assimilated by the Greeks. It is equally feasible that these same remnants, no doubt modified and altered along the way, subsequently formed part of the working practices that are common in astronomy and geometry today. The Phaistos Disc, which lay undisturbed in the ruins of a forgotten palace while classical Greece flourished, may show that only part of the Minoan invention of the original unified system of looking at the universe ever found its way to the city states of Greece.

A mastery of astronomy also meant a mastery over mankind. Such knowledge is not given up lightly and there were probably only a few people on Crete, even in Minoan times, who truly understood what discs like the Phaistos example really had to say. It is possible that as the pillars of Knossos crashed down some time around 1450 BC, the flowering of Minoan mathematical genius lay crushed with the priests and priestesses who took their knowledge with them to the grave. The Phaistos Disc may be the last surviving link with a way of looking at the world that has not seen the light of day for nearly 4,000 years. We are left with only one disc from the Minoan culture, though it is probable that there were originally many of them, all related to the same way of viewing the universe and all based on the same mathematical principles. If they were all made of clay, as the surviving example was, it is not surprising that the other discs have failed to stand the test of time.

Robert Graves, in his excellent book *The White Goddess*, relates the story of a mythical character by the name of Palamedes. Ancient authorities associate Palamedes with Crete. He is supposed to have fought at Troy on the side of the Greeks and was reputed to have been buried on the Mysian coast of Asia Minor, opposite Lesbos. Palamedes is credited with having invented the alphabet, lighthouses, measures, scales and the disc, though it is generally accepted that his inventions are really attributable to ancient Crete. The alphabet could easily relate to the hieroglyphic script used on the Phaistos Disc. Presumably, mention of 'the disc' in this context is meant to imply discs in general. It is not unreasonable to assume that the discs in question actually served some useful purpose. The fact that they are mentioned in context with the other inventions in the list could turn out to be especially significant.

CHAPTER SIX

THE MINOAN
CALENDAR

As mentioned in the previous chapter, the Minoans may have understood that there is more than one way to measure the length of a year. It is almost certain that they understood the idea of the tropical year and they may well have grasped the idea of the sidereal year. These are not the same length. The tropical year is defined as the time taken by the Sun to make two successive passages across the vernal equinox. This sounds more complicated than it is. In fact, it is the length of year that was most easily understood by cultures early in human history. It is often known as the natural year and is 365.2422 days in length. The sidereal year is judged on a different set of criteria. The Minoans would have seen the sidereal year as the time between two successive visits of the Sun to the same point in space, as measured against the backdrop of stars. Since the brightness of the Sun obscures the stars behind it, this cannot be done by observation and this period of time can only be calculated mathematically.

Trying to create a workable calendar, when it is obvious that there are not a whole number of days in the year, must have been something of a headache. A reasonably accurate calendar was essential for any farming culture, since planting and harvesting are tied very closely to the movement of the Sun through the various stages of its north–south passage. However, to a people like the Egyptians, the situation was not too difficult, partly because they did not really need a calendar as such, merely a working knowledge of a certain astronomical event. This was the rising of Sirius.

When the Egyptian civilisation was still young, the astronomers noticed that the star we know as Sirius (the dog-star) was first observed in the evening sky each year only a few days before the flooding of the Nile. It hardly ever rained in Egypt and the economy was based exclusively on farming which in turn owed its existence to the Nile. Clearly, the behaviour of the Nile was fundamental to the continued existence of the Egyptian civilisation along the Nile valley. For this reason, the regular rising of Sirius was the most important astronomical event in Egypt, probably far more so than an accurate understanding of the solar calendar. The Egyptians considered the year to be 360 days in length, adding five extra days at the end of each year as celebration days. Across several thousand years, they never compensated for the extra quarter of a day each year. Nevertheless, they seem to have muddled along quite well, thanks to their highly specific requirements regarding knowledge of when the Nile was going to flood.

However, to a culture like the Minoans, things were very different. They relied heavily on the winter rains and could suffer failures in agriculture if planting did not precede the searing heat of summer by the correct time interval. There have always been many species of food plants grown on Crete and many of these have quite different requirements for successful farming and harvesting. The island is temperate in the north but semi-tropical in the south, with a wide fluctuation in temperature between summer and winter as well as between the fertile plains and the lush pastures to be found among the more arid mountain tracts. Therefore, the rough and ready system favoured by the Egyptians simply would not have been good enough for the Minoans.

It is as valid to overestimate the length of the year by three-quarters of a day, as the Minoans did, as it is to underestimate it by a quarter of a day as we do. Both are simply different ways of dealing with the same problem. In the early days of the Minoan civilisation, it had been discovered that a rectification of a 366-day calendar could be achieved after 40 solar years and again after 480 solar years (12 times 40) and so the 366-day calendar came into use.

Each year was divided into 12 months, the length of successive months alternating between 30 and 31 days. At the end of the year, the Sun would have advanced slightly further than it had done in the tropical solar year, since the Minoan year of 366 days exceeded the tropical year by about three-quarters of a day. After the completion of 40 tropical years and 40 Minoan years, the difference between the number of days which had passed was just over 30 days, a fraction shorter than the average length of a Minoan month.

The Minoan year exceeded the tropical year by 0.7578 of a day to be exact. After the completion of 40 tropical years and 40 Minoan years, the number of days that had passed were 14,609.688 days in the case of tropical years and 14,640 days in the case of Minoan years. The difference between them is 30.312 days. Thus, 40 Minoan years were longer than 40 tropical solar years by 30.312 days which is just short of the mean length of a Minoan month, 30.5 days (the mean is arrived at by adding 30 and 31 and dividing by 2).

Thus, if the Sun had returned to its starting point on a given day 40 years after it was first noted at the same point in the sky, it would have moved forward in the zodiac by one full sign by the time the Minoan Cycle ended (because the Sun takes one month to travel through each sign).

What is important here is that there is a finite and sensible difference between the two calendars, as well as an obvious point of reference at the end of every Minoan Cycle of 40 years.

At the end of 480 years (12 Minoan Cycles of 40 years each), the difference between the two calendars was considerably greater, almost exactly one tropical year.

Here the numbers start to get rather large but they are still manageable. As far as the decimal places are concerned, only the first three need to be considered when thinking about what the numbers mean. Thus, 0.1 is one-tenth, 0.01 is one-hundredth and 0.001 is one-thousandth. It is only when doing calculations that all the decimal places need to be taken into account. There are 175,316.256 days in 480 tropical years and 175,680 days in 480 Minoan years. The difference between them is 363.744 days which is almost exactly one tropical year.

The meeting point between the tropical year and the Minoan year is at its closest at this point, though even after 480 years the tropical and Minoan years still do not coincide exactly; the shortfall is 1.4982 days (about a day and a half).

Because the Sun would be expected to be back at its starting point for the start of the thirteenth Minoan Cycle (Day 1 of the next Grand Minoan Cycle), the Minoan astronomers probably would have extended the last Minoan Cycle by one day or possibly by two days to allow the Sun to occupy the zodiac sign and degree where it started the whole process 480 years earlier. If after one Grand Minoan Cycle one day was added to the calendar for that year and two were added after the next Grand Minoan Cycle, the pattern would remain true to within an incredible 0.0036 of a day – about five minutes after 960 years.

Because accuracy cross-checks were available at 40-year intervals, this does not necessarily mean that the calendar was only rectified after each 40-year period. If this had been the case, days would have started to slip back throughout the year and planting seasons would have become hopelessly confused. The situation could have been handled in one of two ways. The 366-day year could have been used uniformly throughout society and the instruction given to pull back all agriculturally sensitive days by three days every four Minoan years. Alternatively, the populace as a whole simply followed instructions year by year as they were handed down from the more knowledgeable people in the priesthood. The second scenario is probably the more likely since this would keep power for ordering the days in the hands of the élite.

Of course, no calendar this accurate is necessary for the simple requirements of farming and the real reason for this amazing system must lie elsewhere. It can be seen that the advancement of the Sun by one zodiac sign every 40 Minoan years would inevitably bring it back to its starting point after 480 Minoan years or 481 tropical years. Thus both the Sun and the ascendant (that point of the zodiac that is crossing the eastern horizon at any point in time) move onward at a known and calculable rate and could be used to make the system easy to follow and accurate in daily use.

So much for the tropical solar year. In addition to the tropical year, there is another sort of year that the Minoans may have understood. This is the sidereal year which has to be calculated mathematically.

Apart from the hieroglyphics on each side of the Phaistos Disc, there is a line with four dots at the end of each spiral. The dots could easily be taken to be a marker that merely indicates the end of the spiral. However, these dots could have served another purpose. In an alternative system to that described above, the Minoan Cycles could have been used in a different way. In this system, days were counted off the disc in exactly the same way as before. Instead of adding three extra days at the end of the cycle, they added four – represented by the four dots at the end of the spiral. We will call this the Revised Minoan Cycle, which differs from the sidereal year by just over the length of the average Minoan month.

When the cycle was completed after 14,637 days (119 times 123), instead of adding three extra days to make the total up to 14,640 days as in the tropical calendar system, the four dots at the end of the spiral represented days which were added to the total, bringing the Revised Minoan Cycle to 14,641 days. The sidereal year is 365.2564 days in length. In 40 sidereal years there are 14,610.256 days. If this is subtracted from the number of days in the Revised Minoan Cycle, the result is 30.744 days. Once again, this is fairly close to the mean Minoan month of 30.5 days.

There are 175,692 days in 12 Revised Minoan Cycles and 175,323.072 days in 480 sidereal years. At the end of the Revised Grand Minoan Cycle, the difference between 12 Revised Minoan Cycles and 480 sidereal years would have been 368.928 days. This is 3.6716 days (nearly four days) longer than the sidereal year. This time, at the end of the Revised Grand Minoan Cycle, four days would have had to have been subtracted from the calendar. Thus, after 481 sidereal years the calendar would have been out by only a third of a day (0.3284 of a day to be precise, the difference between 4 and 3.6716). This discrepancy would have become about half a day after two Revised Grand Minoan Cycles (which is 962 years). This is much greater than the 5-minute discrepancy in the tropical system. However, the sidereal method of cross-checking the calendars would have had the advantage of using the same basic unit (four days) for making corrections.

At so far a remove from the Minoan civilisation, it is not possible today to be certain which of these systems the Minoans favoured. Both fit neatly into the general scheme of things so it is entirely possible that the Minoans kept a close eye on sidereal cycles as well as the tropical ones, using them for cross-checking the accuracy of their calendar based on the tropical year.

CHAPTER SEVEN

A MATHEMATICAL MACHINE

As a calendar, the Disc worked on different levels, so that, in addition to calculating the passing of the Minoan Cycles, it seems likely that the months of the year were reflected in the phrases. There are 30 phrases on one side of the disc and 31 on the other. However, I think it is unlikely that the days of the month are named in the phrases, mainly because there are so many repeats on side A.

How did the Phaistos Disc work and how was it used? These are fundamental questions that need to be answered. We have seen what *could* be achieved with the Disc but that does not necessarily indicate what the Minoans would have done. Using the mathematical principles that I have discovered in the ordering of the symbols and lines on the Disc, these questions can now be answered with a high degree of certainty. To help you follow the explanations below, you may find it helpful to refer to the illustrations of the Phaistos Disc on pages 32 and 33. The likely purpose of the radial lines that divide the symbols into phrases will be explained later. At this stage, the lines merely serve to confuse the issue. So for the sake of simplicity, we will ignore them for the moment.

On Day 1 of the first Minoan Cycle (which as you will recall lasts for 40 Minoan years), the person consulting the Disc would have used what I have chosen to call side B. (My choice of which side is called A and which is called B has no bearing on the way in which the Disc would have been used by the Minoans. My choice is quite arbitrary and is merely for the sake of easy reference.) At the very centre of the Disc is a small rounded triangle. This symbol is the ruling symbol for the first subcycle of the Minoan Cycle and remains effective for the following 123 days, the number of symbols on side A. In other words, the triangle on side B rules the 123 days of the first subcycle (and consequently each subcycle is 123 days in length). The days are counted off on side A, starting with the flower at its centre. Thus, the triangle on side B together with the flower on side A become Subcycle 1, Day 1 of the Minoan Cycle. This can be expressed as 1:1.

The next day is governed by the next symbol on side A of the Disc. This is a man's head. The triangle on side B of the Disc together with the man's head on side A become Subcycle 1, Day 2 of the Minoan Cycle which can be expressed as 1:2. The third day of the cycle can be read as the triangle on side B in association with the oar symbol on side A. The triangle and the oar become Subcycle 1, Day 3 which can be expressed as 1:3. So the process continues, counting off the symbols on side A one after the other until the last warrior's head on side A of the Disc is reached. This, together with the triangle on side B, represents Subcycle 1, Day 123, or 1:123.

The user of the Disc now returns to side B and refers to the symbol that comes after the triangle. This looks like a strap of some sort. The strap becomes the symbol for the second subcycle of the Minoan Cycle. Once again, the symbols on side A of the Disc are counted off, one after the other, in association with the strap symbol. Thus, the strap and the flower become Subcycle 2, Day 1, or 2:1. One after the other, the symbols on side B of the Disc come into play, each one being counted off against each of the 123 symbols on side A. This continues until, after 14,637 days, the last warrior's head on side B coincides with the last warrior's head on side A at Subcycle 119, Day 123 which can be expressed as 119:123.

It is my belief that at this point three extra days were added in order to bring the total to 14,640 before the next Minoan Cycle was started from the centre of the Disc. These extra days are not indicated on the Disc. You will recall that 14,640 days is 40 years at 366 days per year. The Minoan calendar could be checked at this point, since an observer would be able to see that the Sun is exactly one sign further along the zodiac than it was at the start of the cycle.

Thus, if the cycle started with the Sun at one Minoan degree (1°M) of Aries, it would now be very close to 1°M of Taurus (one Minoan degree is, of course, $\frac{1}{366}$ of a full circle; it is called a

Minoan degree to distinguish it from our sort of degrees one of which is, of course, $\frac{1}{360}$ of a full circle).

Within the duration of one full Minoan Cycle, composed of 40 Minoan Years, the Sun can be seen to travel 40 times round the heavens to end up, not back at its starting point, but one zodiac sign further on. Since there are 12 zodiac signs, it is likely that the Minoans considered that there were 12 of these cycles, the twelfth one of which brought the Sun back to its starting point in the zodiac. As we already know, this happened after 12 Grand Minoan Cycles which corresponded to 481 solar years, the difference between the two systems at this point being only one and a half days. This is the closest that the 366-day year and the 365.2422-day year ever came to each other.

Why had the Minoans used the numbers 123 and 119 for the cycles? There did not seem to be any logic behind the choice of 123 and 119. After all, these two numbers when multiplied together do not total exactly 14,640 days. Why had they not chosen 120 and 122 which do exactly make 14,640 when multiplied together? The answer to this, I believe, lies in the very special properties possessed by the number 123 when viewed through the eyes of the Minoan astronomers and mathematicians. The number 123 has a property which turned the Phaistos Disc into something much more than a calendar.

The signs of the zodiac and the months of the year, which were effectively the same thing in Minoan terms, alternated between 30 and 31; that is, between 30 and 31 *degrees* as far as the zodiac is concerned but between 30 and 31 *days* when dealing with months. The signs of the zodiac and the months of the year were the same because the Sun took alternately 30 and 31 days to pass through each sign. The magic of the number 123 in this context is that it exceeded four signs of the zodiac by just one day. This may not sound particularly significant but it makes a great difference to the calculations.

Since the dawn of astrology, the signs of the zodiac have all been considered to conform to one of four elements: Fire, Earth, Air and Water. The 12 signs as we know them today and the elements which rule them are Aries (Fire), Taurus (Earth), Gemini (Air), Cancer (Water), Leo (Fire), Virgo (Earth), Libra (Air), Scorpio (Water), Sagittarius (Fire), Capricorn (Earth), Aquarius (Air) and

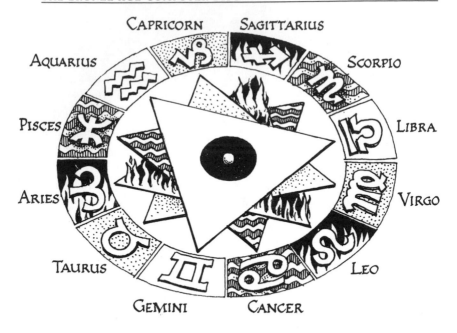

The modern signs of the zodiac represent the
12 divisions of the solar year.

Pisces (Water). Minoan zodiac signs probably had different names and associations because it is known that the names and associations of some of the signs have slightly altered over time.

The interesting thing about the number 123 is that, in terms of days, it represents the passage of the Sun through four signs of the zodiac and its arrival in the next sign on the last day of the subcycle. This means that it ends the 123-day subcycle in the next zodiac sign of the same element. The three signs associated with each element are arranged so that the ordering of the elements is regular which means that the next sign of the same element is always four signs away. For example, if the Sun occupies the first degree of Aries, which is the first Fire sign, at the start of the first subcycle, it completes its journey through Aries, Taurus, Gemini and Cancer, ending the subcycle in the second degree of Leo which is the second Fire sign in the zodiac. From here, it starts the next subcycle. Herein lies the basis of a very efficient way of working out where the Sun is most likely to appear in the sky, not simply on any day but at any hour of the day as well.

If an accurate reading of the Sun's position relative to the zodiac was to be achieved, certain compensations would have had to have been made, however. These compensations need not bother us here: for the moment, we will assume that the Sun actually does travel, in the Minoan system, at exactly one Minoan degree per day. The full calculations including the compensatory adjustments can be found in the next chapter.

After several thousand years it is impossible to know which of the zodiac signs the Minoans considered to be 30°M in length and which 31°M in length. The result would be essentially the same, however, so for our purposes we will assume that to the Minoans the Fire signs (Aries, Leo and Sagittarius) and the Air signs (Gemini, Libra and Aquarius) were all 30°M in length. This would mean that the Earth signs (Taurus, Virgo and Capricorn) and the Water signs (Cancer, Scorpio and Pisces) were all 31°M in length.

Utilising the Minoan system, working out the position of the Sun on any given day merely relies on knowing exactly where the Sun is to be found at the start of any subcycle. This can be ascertained from a simple calculation on the Disc. In effect, the starts of the subcycles form a microcosm of the complete Minoan Cycle, the only difference being that the zodiac signs change, although they remain of the same element.

Reproduced below is a section of the tables that I have drawn up to show this effect. On the left is the position of the Sun in the zodiac sign at the start of each subcycle. On the right is the Sun's actual position during the first subcycle of successive Minoan Cycles. The two are essentially the same, except that the zodiac sign is different for successive subcycles in a given Minoan Cycle.

Sun's position at the start of successive Minoan Subcycles	Sun's position during the first subcycle of successive Minoan Cycles
1°M of Aries	1°M of Aries
2°M of Leo	2°M of Aries
3°M of Sagittarius	3°M of Aries
4°M of Aries	4°M of Aries
5°M of Leo	5°M of Aries
6°M of Sagittarius	6°M of Aries

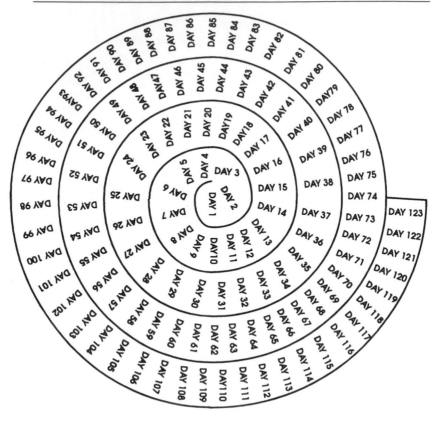

A simple reconstruction of the symbols on side A
of the Phaistos Disc.

In this way, the whole of the Minoan Cycle can be viewed in the first subcycle, the only difference being the changing zodiac sign of the subcycles. Since the zodiac sign will always be related to its companions in a series (in this instance they are all Fire signs), working out where the Sun is in the zodiac at the start of any cycle is really quite simple.

This pattern is easier to follow using a simple reconstruction of the Disc (see pages 70 and 71). Side B of the simple reconstructed Disc (see page 71), shows what position of the zodiac the Sun could be considered to occupy at noon on any day that starts a 123-day subcycle. We assume for the purposes of the exercise that the first subcycle starts with the Sun at 1°M of Aries at noon in Phaistos,

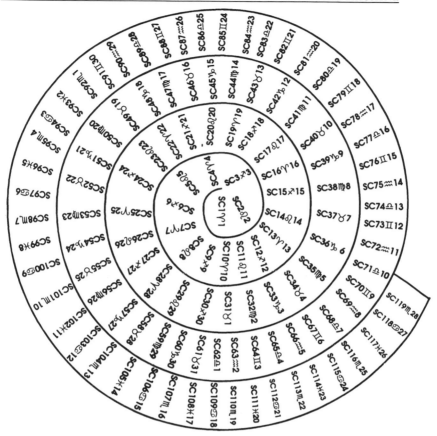

A simple reconstruction of the symbols on side B
of the Phaistos Disc.

KEY:

♈	=	Aries	♎	=	Libra
♉	=	Taurus	♏	=	Scorpio
♊	=	Gemini	♐	=	Sagittarius
♋	=	Cancer	♑	=	Capricorn
♌	=	Leo	♒	=	Aquarius
♍	=	Virgo	♓	=	Pisces
			SC	=	Sub Cycle

Crete. At the same time of day but on the first day of the next subcycle, which would occur 123 days later, the Sun could be expected to occupy 2°M of Leo. Another 123 days on, the Sun will be at 3°M of Sagittarius, while at the start of the fourth subcycle, it will have arrived at 4°M of Aries. Such a straightforward system, albeit shown here in a simplified form, would not be possible with our present method of timekeeping because our year has 365 days (plus a bit) in it, not 366. All that is required as far as the Minoan system is concerned is a careful logging of the days within the Minoan Cycle, together with the exact position of the Sun at the start of the Cycle. If, for example, that starting point is 1°M of Aries, the starts of Subcycles 1 to 30 must all be in the Fire signs, the starts of Subcycles 31 to 61 must all be in the Earth signs, the starts of Subcycles 62 to 91 must all be in the Air signs, and the starts of Subcycles 92 to 119 must all be in the Water signs.

The reason that life is so much more complicated with our present way of watching the skies is because we rely on a 365-day year which is corrected to 365.25 days by adding an extra day every four years. With our system, the Sun does not pass through one degree of arc each day. Because of this, and the changing length of the year as measured from the calendar, the Sun does not necessarily enter any zodiac sign on the same day in any given year and is difficult to track day by day. In the Minoan system, once the position of the Sun at the start of any subcycle is known, it is only necessary to count forward at the rate of one Minoan degree per day on through the zodiac from that point in order to discover the Sun's position on any day within that subcycle.

As an example, let us suppose that we want to know the position of the Sun within the zodiac for Subcycle 2, Day 12. We know that Subcycle 2 must start at 2°M of Leo; this is the first day of the 12 days which we have to move forward. This means that on Day 12 of the subcycle the Sun will be at 13°M of Leo.

I firmly believe that, to the Minoans, this would not simply have been an academic exercise. Knowing the Sun's position at any given time allows all sorts of other calculations to be made. Some of these are important for strictly astronomical reasons; but it is in the field of celestial navigation that an accurate fix on the Sun is of real importance. Knowing the geographic position of the Sun at any hour of any day is the first requirement in celestial navigation and ultimately leads to establishing the position of a vessel on the Earth's surface at any given point in time. Because there are not exactly 366 days in a solar year, even with the Minoan way of looking at timekeeping, the Sun does not move exactly one Minoan degree within the zodiac on any given day.

Its actual movement is about seven Minoan seconds of arc (expressed as 7"M of arc) more than 1°M during a 24-hour period.

In terms of naked-eye observations, there is only a very small discrepancy but over a period as long as the Minoan Cycle (40 Minoan years) it adds up to sizeable figure; without corrections, the discrepancy would amount to around 30 Minoan degrees of arc by the end of a Minoan Cycle.

To make the necessary corrections would not have been difficult and would have been aided by using the lines that divide the phrases on the Phaistos Disc. The Minoans possessed a stunning 'quick reference system' for discovering the position of the Sun on any day that could be said to rival anything invented up to the start of our own technological age. A complete understanding of Minoan genius can only really be appreciated when the beauty and harmony of the 123-day subcycle system is fully understood.

To facilitate a greater understanding of the mathematical principles of the Phaistos Disc, I have created a modern version of this remarkable 'machine'. It is now time to take a look at this modern reconstruction of an ancient wonder.

CHAPTER EIGHT

THE RECONSTRUCTED ASTRONOMICAL DISC

I n the last chapter, we looked at the potential of the number 123 when assessing the position of the Sun within the zodiac on any day during a Minoan Cycle. However, because of the difference between the Minoan year of 366 days and the solar year of 365.2422 days, the Sun does not actually move a full one Minoan degree (1°M) of arc each day. The sun's daily movement is actually about seven Minoan seconds (7″M) of arc more than one Minoan degree (1°M) of arc.

A gain of 7″M presupposes that the Minoans divided one minute of arc into 60 seconds, of course. However, I suspect that the Minoans divided one minute into only six seconds. This difference might complicate our calculations to find the position of the Sun. Fortunately, the way the Phaistos Disc is laid out obviates any difficulties.

On my simple reconstructed disc (see pages 76 and 77), the number system is exactly the same as on the original, except that the symbols have been replaced by astrological signs and numbers. I have also spaced the dissecting lines between the phrases more uniformly, in order to facilitate greater accuracy. I stress that the way in which we are about to use this disc is not how the original Disc was designed to be used; this is clear from the way the pictograms are arranged on the Phaistos Disc. However, the exercise we are about to undertake is still valid, for it will demonstrate the amazing

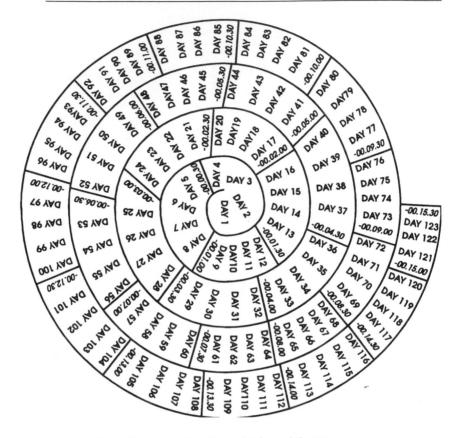

A complex reconstruction of side A of the Disc.

sophistication of Minoan mathematical principles.

Finding the position of the Sun in the zodiac at any point in time is an essential part of determining your location on the Earth's surface. Generally speaking, this is not an easy task, unless you have recourse to a whole series of tables and you are able to do some mathematics which can be confusing and are unfortunately liable to error. It is my contention that the same job, Minoan style, can be achieved in a couple of minutes and with remarkable accuracy. Once the principles are understood, a primary school student would have no difficulty in determining the correct answer.

Before we look at the reconstructed disc, however, we must get to grips with the rules of how to use it; these are fundamental to making it all work but are easily memorised. Armed with these,

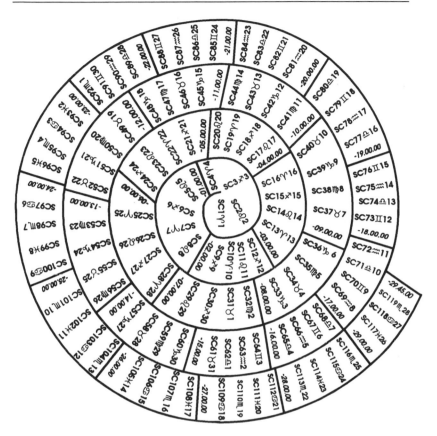

A complex reconstruction of side B of the Disc.

KEY:

♈ =	Aries	♎ =	Libra	
♉ =	Taurus	♏ =	Scorpio	
♊ =	Gemini	♐ =	Sagittarius	
♋ =	Cancer	♑ =	Capricorn	
♌ =	Leo	♒ =	Aquarius	
♍ =	Virgo	♓ =	Pisces	
		SC =	Sub Cycle	

numerous people with no prior knowledge of astronomy have successfully undertaken this exercise. They did not need to understand the mechanism by which the results are derived in order to complete the exercise. Thus it would have been possible to teach the captain of a Minoan ship how to calculate the position of the Sun, wherever his craft happened to be – provided he was reasonably numerate, of course. Once the rules are understood, the disc is not difficult to use, although a little perseverance is required. So, before using the reconstructed disc to establish the true position of the Sun within the zodiac on any given day, it is important to follow the two simple rules given below.

Rule 1

The Minoan Subcycle and the day of the Subcycle must be known.

Rule 2

You must be aware of triplicities. Triplicities are the groups of zodiac signs ruled by a particular element. They are: Fire (Aries, Leo and Sagittarius), Earth (Taurus, Virgo and Capricorn), Air (Gemini, Libra and Aquarius), and Water (Cancer, Scorpio and Pisces). As the year progresses, the pattern of Fire, Earth, Air and Water is repeated through the 12 signs, so that when the period covered by the last of the Water signs, (Pisces), ends, the first of the Fire signs, (Aries), appears again. The sequence is as follows: Aries (Fire), Taurus (Earth), Gemini (Air), Cancer (Water), Leo (Fire), Virgo (Earth), Libra (Air), Scorpio (Water), Sagittarius (Fire), Capricorn (Earth), Aquarius (Air), Pisces (Water).

In any Minoan Cycle there are 14,640 days, so that to produce tables showing the position of the Sun in the zodiac at noon on any particular day takes up masses of tables. What we need is a method that is fast, accurate and depends on only one set of figures. It seems that the Minoans devised such a system. The whole thing relies on the ability to handle numbers in certain ways and upon the magic of the number 123. Within each Minoan Cycle, there are 119 subcycles, each of which is 123 days in length. Our examples define these in the following way: Subcycle 12, Day 24 would be defined as 12:24; Subcycle 102, Day 63 would be defined as 102:63.

Example 1

Let us suppose that you want to know the position of the Sun at noon for Subcycle 23, Day 40 (23:40).

First of all you add the subcycle number, 23, and the day number, 40, which comes to 63. If the number you get when you add the day number and the subcycle number is less than 123, you subtract 1 from the sum of the addition. In this case it is less than 123, so you subtract 1 from 63 to give you 62. Taking the number 62, you look at side B of the reconstructed disc, scanning the numbers on the wheel until you find Subcycle 62. Underneath it, you find a degree number and a zodiac sign. In this case it is 1°M of Libra.

This turns out to be the degree that you are looking for but the triplicity could be wrong. In other words, the answer you want could really be 1°M of Gemini, Libra or Aquarius. To find which is correct, go back to the subcycle and day (23:40) for which you are making the determination. If you look again at the disc, you can see that Subcycle 23 started with the sign of Leo. As you are looking for a result of 1°M of an Air sign and the next Air sign beyond Leo is Libra, your answer is therefore 1°M of Libra.

It is as simple as that.

Example 2

Imagine that you want to know the position of the Sun at noon on Subcycle 96, Day 43 (96:43).

Once again, you add the subcycle and day numbers, 96 and 43 in this case, and this gives you 139. This is higher than 123, so this time you do not subtract 1 from the sum of the addition; instead, you subtract 123 from the sum and 139 minus 123 gives you 16. You now look at side B of the disc. Underneath Subcycle 16 you will find 16°M of Aries. You know that 16°M is right but that the triplicity could be Aries, Leo or Sagittarius. To ascertain which is correct, you look again at the subcycle and day (96:43) for which you are making the determination. Subcycle 96 began with Pisces and the next Fire sign beyond Pisces is Aries. Therefore, the answer is 16°M of Aries.

Example 3

This time suppose that you want to know the noon position of the Sun for Subcycle 12, Day 60 (12:60). As before, add the subcycle and day numbers, 12 and 60, which gives you 72. This number is less than 123 and so you subtract 1 from the sum which gives you 71. Referring to the disc, you will see that 10°M of Libra is below Subcycle 71. To find the correct triplicity, refer to the subcycle and day for which you are doing the determination (12:60). Subcycle 12 started with Sagittarius. The Air sign immediately following Sagittarius is Aquarius. Therefore the answer is 10°M of Aquarius.

79

As long as the two rules are followed, the answer will always be correct.

However, this is only the first part of the procedure we must follow if we want a really accurate determination of the Sun's position at any given time. There are several ways in which the correction can be made. The one used here is the one which the Minoans might well have used because it is easy to remember and therefore easy to use.

Quite simply, we need to add 0.25°M for every subcycle on the disc that comes before the one in which we are interested. Let us look again at Example 3, which concerns Subcycle 12. Since 0.25°M must be added for every subcycle that comes before Subcycle 12, we need to multiply 0.25°M by 11 (because there are 11 subcycles before Subcycle 12) and add the result of this multiplication. The multiplication works out at 2.75°M or 2°M 45'M (one Minoan minute is expressed as 1'M). This is added to the original answer of 10°M of Aquarius. The result is 12°M 45'M of Aquarius. Our assessment of the Sun's position in this case is now accurate to within a maximum error of 1.5'M of arc. This is pretty good going for a Bronze Age culture. And yet we can gain an even greater degree of accuracy still if we wish.

Look on side A of the disc, where the day numbers within the subcycles are shown. To get truly amazing accuracy, we need to count forward the exact number of days within the subcycle in our example, Subcycle 12, Day 60. To make the right compensation for the day we are interested in, we have to add 3"M of arc for every four days. To make this easier, you can count the radial lines that cross the disc, starting from the centre, since they appear every four days. Alternatively, you can simply divide 60 by 4, which comes out as 15. Multiplying 15 by 3"M gives us 45"M. We add this to the previous figure of 12°M 45'M of Aquarius and the answer is 12°M 52'M 3"M of Aquarius. We now know the exact position of the Sun within the zodiac at noon on Subcycle 12, Day 60.

Example 4

Assume that you want to know the position of the Sun at noon on Subcycle 7, Day 45 (7:45).

Add the subcycle and day numbers, 7 and 45, and this comes to 52. Since this is less than 123, subtract 1 from 52 which gives you 51. Look at side B of the reconstructed disc and you will see that beneath Subcycle 51 is 21°M of Capricorn. Capricorn may not be the correct triplicity, so refer to the subcycle and day for which you are doing the determination (7:45). This subcycle starts with the sign of Aries. The next Earth sign after Aries is Taurus and so the answer must be 21°M of Taurus. There are six subcycles before Subcycle 7. Multiplying 0.25°M by 6 gives you 1°M 30'M. Add this to 21°M and this gives 22°M 30'M of Taurus.

The day number is 45. Dividing 45 by 4 comes to 11 with 1 remaining. Multiply 11 by 3″M and this comes to 33″M. If you wish, you can also add 7″M for the remaining day of the 45, though even by modern standards this is unnecessary. Add 33″M to 22°M 30'M and this gives you the position of the Sun at noon, namely 22°M 35'M 3″M of Taurus.

This then is the full method of using the reconstructed disc.

Once the principles are understood, there are many ways to speed up the procedure. The lines that divide the numbers on both sides of the disc into sections can be used as counting markers, and it is easily remembered what increment has to be made for the corrections, since the number 4 is operative, both in terms of subcycles and in terms of days. For subcycles, 1°M is added for every four subcycles, while for days, 3″M are added for every four days. To make matters even easier, I have added the expected correction after each dividing line on both sides of the disc.

Of course, it may not be noon on the day on which you want to find the position of the Sun. However, we know that according to the Minoan method the Sun travels 1°M plus 7″M within the zodiac every day. The Minoan day is split into 12 Minoan hours and this means that the Sun travels at 5'M per Minoan hour within the zodiac; alternatively, if our 24-hour day is the frame of reference, the Sun travels at 2.5'M per hour. So for every hour, we simply add or subtract (depending on whether the hours come before noon or after noon) the appropriate number of Minoan minutes to correct the calculations.

Did the Minoans use a system such as this one to correct the position of the Sun for any hour or any day within their cycles? It is entirely possible, for this was a truly remarkable people.

CHAPTER NINE

TRACKING THE INNER PLANETS

U
nlike earlier generations, we cannot look up into the
night sky and see the stars picked out clearly against the
black backdrop of space. Light from present-day
conurbations spills into the night sky reducing the blackness so that
only the brightest stars can be seen easily. This is why the big optical
telescopes are sited in remote parts of the world and preferably
high up – to get away from the huge amount of light that our
modern society produces. Even in the countryside the all-
pervading spill of light cannot be avoided, although it is a little less
strong. Before the advent of electric light, there was no diminution
of the blackness of the night sky and on a clear night anyone could
marvel at the planets and the stars without a telescope, using only
the naked eye.

Of course, in Minoan times there was no such pollution of the
night sky. There were no conurbations and no electric light. The
night was truly black. As a consequence, the Minoans and their
contemporaries could see much more of the heavens with the
naked eye than we can today. How did they view the heavens and
what exactly could they see of our solar system? Although we now
know how the planets and their moons, the asteroids and the
comets are arranged within the solar system, early people did not.
For one thing, they were not aware of the presence of all the
planets. Pluto, for example, was not discovered until the 1930s.
Until relatively recently, the solar system stopped at Saturn.

The solar system has the Sun at its centre, although it is highly
improbable that the Minoans saw the Sun as something around
which the Earth orbited. They no doubt believed that the Earth was

stationary and the orb of the Sun moved across the sky, because to an observer on Earth that is what appears to happen; and we are not aware of the Earth's movement in space even when we know that it is moving in space at quite a speed. Apart from the other planets in the solar system, there are asteroids and other debris as well as comets. All the members of this family travel around the Sun in their own individual orbits. While the gravity of the Sun seeks to pull these various bodies in towards itself, the centrifugal force that acts on all of them by virtue of their motion round the Sun tries to hurl them out of their orbits and into space. These two forces are in equilibrium – otherwise, one of them would win the contest and, in the case of the Earth for example, the planet would either plunge into the Sun or hurtle out into space with the inevitable result in either instance that all life on the planet would cease.

Without the Sun there would be no life on Earth, of course. The Sun not only keeps our world in a more or less fixed orbit but also provides heat and light, two of the necessities of all living things. And water, which of course is also essential to life, would not fall as rain without the sun.

The Sun is a vast ball of burning gases, mainly hydrogen and helium. It is approximately 865,000 miles across and about 93,000,000 miles from Earth. In the central core of the Sun, fusion of hydrogen atoms into helium atoms generates huge amounts of energy so that it is unbelievably hot, about 15,000,000°C, although the surface is much cooler at about 6,000°C. The Sun consumes 5,000,000 tonnes of matter every second, releasing 3×10^{26} watts of energy – that is 3 followed by 26 noughts or 300 million million million million. It is middle-aged, about 5 billion years old, and not so different from many of the other stars in our galaxy although it is, in fact, one of the smallest stars. There are an estimated 100 billion stars in our galaxy, which is not an especially large one.

Working out from the centre of the solar system, the nearest planet to the Sun is Mercury. Then comes Venus. Beyond Venus is the Earth. Because Mercury and Venus lie between the Earth and the Sun they are known as 'inferior' planets. All heavenly bodies further out than the Earth are known as 'superior' planets. Beyond the Earth is Mars which is about half the diameter of our own planet. Then comes Jupiter, the biggest of the super-giants. Saturn, Uranus and Neptune are next and finally there is little Pluto.

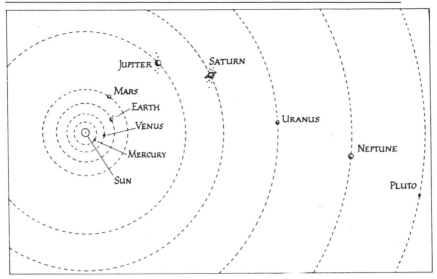

***The planets of our solar system in their orbits
around the Sun.***

Between Mars and Jupiter lies a belt of asteroids made up of large and small rocks which may have made up a planet at some time in the distant past.

Many of the planets also have families of their own. Mars, for example, has two moons while our own planet has one. The super-giants have many moons. Because the moons orbit their host planets and travel through space along with them as the planets orbit the Sun, the orbits of the moons are more like flattened spirals. In addition to the planets, the Sun also has a family of comets. A comet is an accumulation of debris and ice, which heats up as it approaches the Sun and often develops a long and beautiful tail which always points away from the sun. Some comets have vast orbits, much more elliptical than those of the planets. Many of them can take centuries to complete just one orbit.

The path taken by the Earth in its orbit around the Sun defines what is called the plane of the ecliptic. An imaginary disc projected out into space from the Earth's equator is known as the celestial equator. Because the Earth is tilted at an angle of about 23.5 degrees from the vertical relative to the ecliptic plane, the plane of the ecliptic and the celestial equator cannot coincide. The angle between the two is known as the obliquity of the ecliptic and is the reason for seasons on the Earth. At different parts of the Earth's orbit, certain areas of the Earth's surface receive more direct sunlight than others. The sunlight is spread over a smaller area and when this happens the Sun can be seen to rise higher in the sky and so warms that particular part of the Earth for longer than if it was lower in the sky.

The belief that the Earth was fixed in space and that everything revolved round the Earth was a convenient way of looking at things. After all these centuries we cannot be certain about how much of the solar system's mechanics was understood by the Minoans. However, it is almost certain that they knew the Earth was round rather than flat. They may also have had some idea that the Earth was not at the centre of the universe but that the Sun was. There is no doubt, however, that they regarded the Sun as an important entity.

When viewed from the Earth, the planets of the solar system, the Sun and the Moon all appear to travel from east to west, keeping more or less to the plane of the ecliptic. Planets can be distinguished from the stars because their light is steadier – they do not twinkle – and because over a period of time they change their position relative to what are known as the 'fixed' stars. It was because of this apparent wandering about the heavens that the term 'planet' was coined and indicates that early civilisations understood the difference between the planets and the stars – planets moved but stars did not.

Because Mercury and Venus lie between the Earth and the Sun, they never appear to wander far from the Sun. Consequently, they can only be seen early in the morning or in the early evening when the sun's brightness does not envelop them. It is technically possible to see Venus during the day but it is very difficult to find and it must be at its brightest if it is to be seen in broad daylight. However, it is unlikely that the Minoans would have been able to identify the planet during the day. The superior planets have vast orbits, millions of miles further out into space than the Earth's. The largest of the planets, Jupiter, takes nearly 12 Earth years to orbit the Sun while distant Pluto, said by some not to be a true planet at all, takes centuries to complete its lonely journey.

Because all the planets travel within the same band of space, they are quite easy to track. However, in order to do this you need a reliable measuring system. Fortunately, the random distribution of stars in the sky can be remembered in terms of the patterns they form. Two such patterns or constellations that many people are familiar with are the 'W' of Cassiopeia and the Big Dipper, also known as the Plough, or more properly Ursa Major, the Great Bear. There are also constellations within the band of space known as the ecliptic and these have a special significance because it is in front of these that the planets can be observed to travel. As demonstrated earlier, at least some modern astronomers think that the Minoans were the first to notice these constellations and name them. We know this pattern of 12 constellations which run round the 360 degrees of the sky as the zodiac.

Once a particular fixed star is recognised within the zodiac, it becomes possible to judge the time for any heavenly body to pass across it. A planet can 'occult' a star, which means that its own bulk blots out the star altogether as it passes in front of it. Alternatively, it can be seen to cross an imaginary line drawn between two convenient stars. By counting the number of days that it takes to reach the same position again, it is possible to calculate how long it takes for the planet to complete an orbit, though the position of the Earth will also have a bearing on such calculations because it will have changed too.

There must have been many aspects of the solar system that ancient peoples like the Minoans did not understand, such as the habit of planets to run apparently 'retrograde' or backwards across the zodiac. This is an effect caused because the Earth and the other planets move relative to each other in orbits of different sizes. Thus, when the orbits of two planets bring them close together, they are travelling in the same direction relative to each other; but when their orbits take them much further apart, so that one of them is on the opposite side of its orbit relative to the other planet, they are travelling in opposite directions relative to each other. This is an illusion, of course, in which circular motion is interpreted as linear motion. This apparent change of direction was one of the clues that eventually led astronomers to realise that the Earth was not the centre of the solar system.

The Moon has a special relationship with the Earth, since it does not orbit the Sun as a planet in its own right but does so as a consequence of its relationship with the Earth. The pattern of the lunar phases is a phenomenon caused by the differing amount of the Moon's sunlit half that can be seen at any time from our own position in space. Lunar phases seem to have always fascinated man and have been studied for a long time. However, plotting the changing position of the Moon day by day is notoriously difficult and must have represented quite a problem to early cultures. Like the Sun, it can be used in celestial navigation but it is rather less reliable without a good understanding of its movements.

Each of the planets was eventually given a name and associated with a personality relevant to the culture observing them. Our ancestors accredited rulership of the solar system, and therefore of the gods, to the planet we now know as Jupiter. Jupiter is an impressive sight, especially on a moon-dark night. Of course, we observe it at a great distance and, in fact, it is so large that it exceeds the mass of all the other planets put together. Jupiter was the name given to the planet by the Romans. To the Greeks, it was known as Zeus. Zeus was the undisputed ruler of the pantheon and was revered as the sky god. The divorcing of astronomy, the scientific study of the heavens, from astrology, which is based on the belief that the heavenly bodies have tangible effects on the Earth and its inhabitants, happened relatively recently. Before the late Middle Ages, the two disciplines were synonymous, so we should not assume that ancient cultures viewed the heavens in the same way as we do today. Proto-astronomy was an amalgam of observation, ritual, mythology and magic. No single part of all this was any more important than the others. However, the numbers formed by the mathematics of planetary interplay had a special significance of their own and, since some patterns were replicable over long periods of time, the power of the gods could be observed in them at first hand.

With time, richer and richer patterns of mythology became associated with all the constellations. Events, real or imagined, were translated into the magical, with heroes and deities alike being transposed from fireside epics to positions among the stars. It is entirely feasible that many of these story cycles started in Crete. It is known that at least some of the Greek gods and goddesses originated on the island. There is a cave, high in the Dikte Mountains, where Zeus is said to have been born and raised. It is also considered that the original Earth goddess may have owed

A goddess idol discovered at Gazi.

much to Minoan Crete. This is particularly true of the more nature-centred versions of the Earth goddess preserved in Greek mythology.

When carrying out research of this nature, it is important to remain objective and not resort to bending the facts to suit the theory. There have been many books written about the Great Pyramid in Egypt, for example, the mathematics of which have been tortured beyond belief to fit each writer's personal preconceptions. The conclusions as to the purpose of the structure have been many and varied, and researchers have gone to great lengths to demonstrate the truth of their own particular views. There is even a story about an early researcher who was discovered filing down his brass measuring rods on site to make the pyramid fit his mathematical expectations of it.

The Phaistos Disc and all that springs from its numbering system is not like the varied theories concerning the Great Pyramid, for it requires no manipulation of the facts – or measuring rods – to show that here is a system that has been meticulously thought out, possibly across centuries, and which conforms wonderfully to the turning Earth and the planets – or at least to those that were known in Minoan times. When you also bear in mind the rich vein of evidence that exists in legend, archaeology, geometry and mathematics, much of which supports the theory, there is little surprise when new and pertinent supportive facts turn up.

One such discovery may explain, in part at least, how the evolution of this Bronze Age view of space and the physical world first came into being. It derives from an early desire to plot the movements of some of the known planets. The two planets in question are known to have been of particular interest to many early civilisations. They are Mercury and Venus. Because Mercury is the innermost of the planets and so close to the Sun, it is often very difficult to spot, though it is visible with the naked eye at dawn or dusk when the Sun is low in the sky. Venus is sometimes hard to find for much the same reason, although it is somewhat easier to see with the naked eye than Mercury because it is closer to the Earth. Because, like Mercury, it is most easily seen at dawn or dusk it became known as the morning or evening star and is arguably one of the most beautiful sights in the sky. Although both Mercury and Venus seem to have held a special place in the beliefs of many ancient cultures, Venus seems to have especially held their fascination.

The orbits of Mercury and Venus take 87.97 days and 224.7 days respectively. The speed of these orbits, together with the orbital path of our own planet, makes the activity of Mercury and Venus somewhat difficult to predict. This is not to say that very early civilisations failed to understand the behaviour of the two planets, though this would obviously have been much easier if there had been a readily discernible repeating pattern that was easy to follow when tracking the relationship which Mercury and Venus keep with the Sun as well as with each other. It seems almost certain that the Minoans discovered a foolproof way of finding the positions of both Mercury and Venus, and of ascertaining when they could be expected to be significantly positioned, such as a conjunction between Mercury and Venus or between one of the planets and the sun. (A conjunction happens when the Sun and the planet in question occupy the same degree of the zodiac when viewed from the Earth. Similarly, a conjunction occurs when two planets occupy the same degree of the zodiac.)

It tends to be taken for granted nowadays that in order to ascertain the position of any planet you simply refer to a book known as an ephemeris in which all such information is recorded for each day in any given year. There is no need for you to make your own observations or to do the necessary calculations. Even if you had to undertake some calculations, there are computers to help you. Perhaps these facts blind us to the tremendous weight of knowledge that was amassed by making observations simply with the naked eye and primitive telescopes. Observations can only be made if there is no cloud and there are certain astronomical events that have to be assumed to happen, rather than actually observed. For example, during any conjunction between the Sun and Mercury or Venus, the planet in question is not visible. The reason for this is quite simple. The Sun is so bright that without sophisticated modern equipment to compensate for the intensity of the light, you cannot safely look at a body passing across its surface. If you tried, you would damage your eyes. Moreover, half of these conjunctions take place with the planet behind the Sun so that you could not possibly see it.

If the Earth occupied a fixed point relative to the Sun, the patterns to look out for would be relatively simple to catalogue. It could be observed that Mercury, with its 88-day orbit, would conjoin with the Sun every 44 days or so, with one conjunction taking place in front of the solar disc and the other taking place behind it. Similarly, Venus would conjoin with the Sun about every 112 days. Unfortunately, the situation is very much more complicated than this because the Earth is also orbiting the Sun. This means that our frame of reference is constantly changing. Thus at first sight the pattern of conjunctions between the two innermost planets and the Sun, and their relationship with each other, appear to be random happenings.

Nevertheless, there *are* patterns to be seen, even if you have to sit around for a considerable period of time in order to make any real sense of them. In the case of Mercury and Venus, I discovered some of these patterns as a direct result of the number systems which may have been at least partly instrumental in the evolution of Minoan geometry. There seems to be a significance to Minoan mathematics that reflects in part the way in which the solar system works. I have no doubt that the Minoans knew about the patterns of the Sun, Mercury and Venus but it is uncertain whether this came about as a result of their using the mathematics and geometry that they had already devised or whether the mathematics and geometry came about as a result of their discovery of the patterns of the Sun, Mercury and Venus.

There is a simple relationship between the orbital periods of the three innermost planets: 166 Mercury orbits take roughly the same length of time as 65 Venus orbits and 40 Earth orbits. This may be part of the reason for the significance of the number 40 to many ancient civilisations. The Minoan system allows accurate predictions to be based on this relationship.

The relationship can best be illustrated by an example. On 9 February 1922, Venus was in conjunction with the Sun at 20° of the sign of Aquarius. Many such conjunctions took place in the years preceding 1922 but the one that is of particular interest to us occurred on 19 February 1882, this time at 0° of the sign of Pisces. The interval between these two conjunctions was 14,600 days. This is exactly 40 days short of one Minoan Cycle of 14,640 days (which is also, of course, 40 Minoan 366-day years). How wonderful, I thought, if this was not simply a one-off coincidence, for what could be easier when tracking the relative positions of the Sun and Venus than counting forward 40 Minoan years and then counting back 40 days? The pattern is easy to follow and would have made a lot of sense to the Minoan astronomers.

Remarkably, this pattern not only works with the relative positions of the Sun and Venus but also with the Sun and Mercury as well as with Mercury and Venus. What is more, it seems that the number 14,637, the product of multiplying 123 by 119 (respectively, the numbers of pictograms on side A and side B of the Disc), is also very important in this regard, especially in connection with Venus. The reason for this lies in the fact that the replay of any aspect formed between the Sun and Venus comes roughly within the three-day period between 14,597 and 14,600 days. The first of these numbers represents 14,637 minus 40 days and the second represents 14,640 minus 40 days (the number of days in a Minoan Cycle of 40 Minoan years minus 40 days). Mercury tends to stick closer to the 14,600 rule, sometimes even extending it by a day or two. In the many examples I have worked through, it never exceeds the 14,600 rule by more than this.

This general rule is applicable to almost any aspect of the relationship between the two innermost planets and the Sun, with Mercury following the true pattern of 40 Minoan years minus 40 days to within a day or two either way and Venus staying closer to three days earlier. What is more, there is always a relationship between the sign and degree of the zodiac where any particular event took place and the position in which the replication of the event will subsequently take place. In each case, the position moves back in the zodiac by a measured number of degrees.

Let us look at times when Mercury was at its greatest elongation (as far away from the Sun as it can get when viewed from the Earth) in successive parts of a Minoan Cycle. Below are four 'pairs' of such events that took place in two successive Minoan Cycles, with the number of days that elapsed between the events, a measurement of the elongation and the number of zodiac degrees between the events.

Date of Mercury's greatest elongation	Position at elongation	Degree and sign at elongation
3 March 1920	18° 119 East	0° 489 Aries
24 February 1960	18° East	22° 59 Pisces
14,602 days		9°
17 April 1920	27° 319 West	29° 459 Pisces
7 April 1960	28° West	19° 589 Pisces
14,600 days		10°
29 June 1920	25° 419 East	3° 069 Leo
19 June 1960	25° East	23° 059 Cancer
14,600 days		10°
14August 1920	18° 429 West	2° 429 Leo
5 August 1960	19° West	23° 559 Cancer
14,601 days		9°

If this process is continued, the average number of days between the greatest elongation of Mercury in one Minoan Cycle and the next is 14,600.5 days and the average number of degrees between the events is ten. Add 40 days to the daily average and the result is 14,640.5 days which is within half a day of 40 Minoan years or 14,640 days.

The same sort of pattern can be laid down for the greatest elongations of Venus.

The results come out at an average of 14,598.3 days apart and about 11° between the events. Add 40 days to the daily average and the result is 14,638 days which is within a day of 14,637 days.

I have not been able to find a relationship between any of these three bodies that does not conform to this pattern, even across vast periods of time. The figures hold together remarkably well and there is no doubt that between the numbers 14,597 and 14,600 (14,640 minus 40 days), we find the replicating patterns of planetary angles and interaction that would have made a simple job of keeping track of the inner planets.

Another very interesting fact, and one that seems unlikely to have been missed by the Minoan astronomers, is that the Sun, Mercury and Venus, having been plotted within the zodiac at the start of a Minoan Cycle, will be seen to reach the same degree of the zodiac at 14,637 minus 30 days. This is especially true of Venus, though slightly less so in the case of Mercury which, although generally true to the pattern, does waver from it by a couple of days either side of the expected date. Venus is much more cooperative, deviating by no more than about half a day from the expected pattern and even then only in about 25 per cent of the many examples I have run on the computer. The fact that the planets behave in this way is not surprising as it is a mathematical consequence of their orbits. To the Minoans, this would have been an important rule of thumb because this pattern is not only to be observed on the first day of a Minoan Cycle but on any day that you choose. Thus, once again, patient observation and cataloguing during one Minoan Cycle ultimately leads to accurate prediction of planetary happenings within other cycles.

Because the Phaistos Disc is essentially governed by the 14,637-day principle, it is possible that in some way it represents a map of Venus's activity during a Minoan Cycle. Much more work would be necessary to ascertain if this is indeed the case. A starting point for Venus would be the most difficult thing to discover. However, I have my doubts because, although Venus holds to the 14,637-day pattern of behaviour very well, it does not appear to follow a 123-day pattern which would also seem to be necessary.

But how would all this have been viewed by the Minoan astronomer priests? I think in order to understand the way that the system might have looked to them, it is important to remember that to the peoples of the Bronze Age no event was of purely mathematical or scientific interest. Each observable cycle of the heavens was merely another manifestation of the proof of the presence of the gods in the grander scheme of things. Here again was the unit of 40 and now of one of 30 which, both in terms of Minoan years and days, allowed them to keep an accurate track of Mercury and Venus. The instructions for doing so are simple and concise, and as long as the day-to-day details of one Minoan Cycle are known, so are all others. This was surely proof positive, to them, of divine intervention in the affairs of humanity.

These examples surely prove how effective and useful the period covered by the Minoan Cycle was when studying astronomical phenomena associated with the Earth and some of its most immediate planetary neighbours. A puzzling question remains, however. Were the 14,640 and 14,637 patterns derived from observation of heavenly phenomena or were they derived directly from the 366-day year adopted by the Minoans? We may never be able to answer this question, though in terms of linear measurement it appears that the Minoans used both numbers with equal ease.

CHAPTER TEN

MINOAN GEOMETRY

Almost as soon as I began to see the Phaistos Disc as a mathematical machine, it started to dawn on me that the implications of this could extend far beyond the Disc being merely a simple means of ordering the calendar. While on one level the Disc could be used quite adequately for counting off the days in each Minoan Cycle, it could also work on a microcosmic level for other purposes. In order to explain what I mean, we must take a slight detour to examine a number of important ideas related to the understanding of the principles involved. Firstly, let us look at the way in which the day is divided up into segments: time and its measurement.

There are two distinctly different aspects of Earth movement that must be understood if an accurate assessment of the passage of time is to be achieved. Firstly, the Earth revolves round the Sun once every year. A Minoan would have seen this as the solar disc passing through each sign of the zodiac in turn during the course of one year. Secondly, the Earth completes a full revolution about its own axis once every day. From a Minoan point of view, the heavens would have passed across any fixed point on the Earth's surface, such as a mountain, for example, once every day.

As surely as the year can be divided up by observing which signs of the zodiac the Sun occupies month by month, so the day can be similarly divided by observing which sign of the zodiac is passing across the eastern horizon at any point in time. Since there are 12 signs in the zodiac and therefore 12 months in the year, it would be a logical step to divide the day into 12 segments as well. The length of each segment could be deduced from how long it took for the Sun to travel across the heavens during the day and from the passing of the observable zodiac constellations over the eastern horizon at night.

Somewhere along the twisted path of history, the number of segments in the day was doubled to produce a 24-hour day, perhaps to allow the daytime and the night-time each to be 12 hours long. Whenever this step was taken, those instigating the change failed to understand the true astronomical significance of a 12-hour day. The 'as above, so below' view of the world was one that was much favoured by early cultures. Dividing the day into 12 segments, as a reflection of the year which also had 12 segments, would probably have had a ritual significance as well as a practical meaning to people who saw all celestial phenomena as evidence of their gods' omnipresence. There seems to be no logical reason for a 24-hour day. Under this system of measurement, each sign of the zodiac takes two hours to clear the eastern horizon and the 24-hour day also breaks the simple but effective connection between the observable events overhead and the passage of time on the Earth.

Secondly, we should take a look at geometry and circles, for it seemed to me that there was an exciting possibility that the Minoans were responsible for developing an early form of geometry that may have laid the foundations for what we understand as geometry today. Having decided that there should be 366 days in a year, the Minoan astronomers laid down the ground rules for a 366-degree circle. It began to look as though the first geometry had therefore been based on a 366-degree circle, rather than the 360-degree circle we use today, and that it had originated as a measurement of time in terms of defining the day and the year. Thus, if the year was split up into 366 days, then each day could be divided into 366 divisions, segments which we now know as degrees.

There is almost certainly a celestial association with the number of degrees in a circle. We know that the Egyptians chose to celebrate a 360-day year, leaving the remaining days as holidays. It is also certain that the peoples of the Nile were accomplished mathematicians. They must have realised from early in their history that 360 is a very convenient number, since it can be divided neatly by so many smaller numbers. Most authorities on early mathematics seem to ignore the origin of the 360-degree circle altogether. Where the subject is touched on, none of the explanations put forward for the adoption of 360 degrees is at all convincing. It seems to me that there is strong circumstantial evidence to suggest that the 360-degree circle originated in Egypt and was subsequently passed down to us via the Greeks and very likely the Arabs, from both of whom so much mathematical knowledge is derived. The number 360 is admirable for the job it has to do. Of necessity, it has long since been separated from its celestial origins. However, the present way of dividing up the circle does relate to the passage of time; although angular measurement and the measurement of time are no longer directly related, the same words are used to describe the divisions of both – minutes and seconds.

We all learned at school that in geometry the degree is split into 60 sections known as minutes of arc and that the minute of arc is split into 60 sections which are known as seconds of arc. In his book on celestial navigation, *Sky and Sextant*, the author John P. Budlong states: 'I've never met the gentleman who gave the same name – minute – to both angle measurements and time measurements. He may have been a mathematician; he certainly wasn't a navigator. The double meaning of one term is a sure source of confusion.' How right Mr Budlong is. How many vessels have come to grief as a result of a confusion over which sort of minute was meant whenever minutes were mentioned? Things may not have always been this way, however. It is more than likely that at the birth of geometry, minutes and seconds of arc were exactly the same thing as minutes and seconds of time. This is the system implied by the numbers used on the Phaistos Disc.

The implications of this are far-reaching. If the Minoans saw the Sun as essentially travelling one Minoan degree within the zodiac in any one day, then they must have realised that the 366 Minoan degrees of the Earth's rotation was equal to one Minoan degree of the sun's passage within the zodiac. It would have therefore been quite easy for them to conclude that during the time it took for one full zodiac sign to pass across the eastern horizon, the Sun would move within the zodiac one Minoan degree (1°M) divided by 12 which is five Minoan minutes (5'M), as we have already seen. The Minoans' use of the Minoan Cycles was a means of keeping a check on the solar year which the Minoans knew was not composed of exactly 366 days. They also knew that the solar year made a bad mathematical model upon which to base their measurements.

However, I was left with something of a puzzle. If the historical evidence pointed to a system which allowed the Minoans to divide the circle so finely, what possible reason could they have had for wanting to divide it in the first place? The time it takes for one Minoan second of arc to be traversed is incredibly short – about 0.065 seconds. In practical terms, anything less than half a second is meaningless for most people; 0.065 seconds is merely a few thousandths of a second. Clearly, 0.065 seconds would have meant as little to the Minoans as it does to us. Even in spatial terms, one Minoan second is difficult to measure with the naked eye – and the Minoans had no telescopes and would have had to make all of their measurements by eye alone. Seconds of arc and probably even minutes of arc are of no consequence when you only have the naked eye for making astronomical observations.

Then suddenly it came to me: it was neither time nor angles that the Minoans sought to measure, it was distance. This was an astonishing discovery and I realised that it could revolutionise the way in which we view the capabilities of Bronze Age cultures.

CHAPTER ELEVEN

THE MINOANS AND THE MEGALITHS

L ittle could I have imagined, on that day in sunny Crete when I saw the Phaistos Disc for the first time, that the solution to one of its fundamental secrets lay back in England. What is more, it turned out to be connected with something that had fascinated me almost from childhood.

My first visit to a megalithic monument was when I was about eight or nine years of age. I was on holiday with my parents in the south of England and we were within striking distance of Stonehenge which stands on the thin, chalky soil of Salisbury Plain in Wiltshire. Out there, in the middle of that often brooding space, the cold stones stand menacing and magical against the backdrop of the rolling green that stretches out beyond. There is something 'other-worldly' about most megalithic monuments and Stonehenge is no exception. It is undoubtedly the most impressive of them all. I remember standing transfixed, looking with the wonder that only a child can feel at those massive balancing sarsen stones and asking myself even then why anyone would want to build something such as this structure, way out here in the middle of nowhere. These first impressions never left me. Since then, I have seen the best of the megalithic monuments that this part of the world has to offer, from the delicate 'fairy rings' of my own Yorkshire Moors, to the towering monoliths of Scotland and Ireland. The most beautiful of them all is the standing stone circle of Castle Rigg in the English Lake District, where the backdrop of the mournful, stunning mountains frames a site that is still alive with mystery.

But how could all these thousands of monuments, from the

furthest reaches of western Ireland to the unbelievable avenues of Brittany in France, have any connection with a culture many hundreds of miles away, south of ancient Greece and close to the northern shores of the African continent? There is an association and it turns out to be a very strong one. Knowledge of this connection comes to us via the long, painstaking work of a man by the name of Alexander Thom.

Alexander Thom was a professor of engineering at Oxford University in England. From the 1930s onward, he had shown an interest in megalithic monuments in Great Britain. Over a period of time, he surveyed hundreds, if not thousands, of these sites and gradually came to the conclusion that there were some definite links between them, most noticeably associated with the system of measurement that had gone into their construction. He ultimately discovered that most sites were built on a basic unit of measurement that he chose to call the megalithic yard. He concluded that this was 2.722 feet in length and that multiples of this measurement could be observed in almost all megalithic sites, from the very earliest to the most recent. Examples of measurements very close to the megalithic yard still exist in parts of Western Europe, India and, surprisingly perhaps, in Central America as well.

For all his painstaking efforts, Professor Thom has certainly had his critics through the years. How, the sceptics wanted to know, could a unit of measurement so precise be expected to survive over a period of 3,000 or more years and across the geographical distances involved, without becoming corrupted or even radically altered on the way? Despite the doubters, the work continued and the weight of evidence is now so strong that the existence of the megalithic yard can hardly be doubted. Fine measurements of carvings, such as the 'cup and ring' and 'spiral' carvings on rocks all over Britain, led Professor Thom to the recognition of a smaller unit of measurement which became known as the megalithic inch. There were, Professor Thom showed, 40 megalithic inches to the megalithic yard.

Was there a connection between the Minoan way of looking at the world and the megalithic monuments of Britain? It was an intriguing possibility. Bearing in mind the frequent use of the number 40 in Minoan mathematics, I thought that it might be worth looking at the megalithic measurements in Minoan terms. What I discovered stunned me.

The nautical mile is a 'stretched' version of the statute mile, the advantage of which is that it allows one minute of arc round the circumference of the Earth to equal one nautical mile. This means that one degree of arc comes out at 60 nautical miles which makes calculations in celestial navigation very much easier than would otherwise be the case. In this respect, the nautical mile is a sensibly defined segment of the Earth's circumference, which the statute mile is not. It is my contention that the inventors of the megalithic yard achieved the same objective of a sensible association between distance and angles several thousand years before the modern invention of the nautical mile.

It must be remembered that to the Minoans any circle contained 366 degrees and not the 360 degrees we know today. If we assume they defined 36.6 megalithic yards as the distance round the Earth of one Minoan second of arc, then this means that the Minoan minute of arc would come out as 60 times 36.6 megalithic yards, which is 2,196 megalithic yards. In terms of statute miles, this is about 1.132 miles. In deference to Professor Thom, I have named this unit the megalithic mile. The megalithic mile is so close to the statute mile that there may, in fact, be some historical relationship between the two measurements. The statute mile is supposed to have been derived from 1,000 Roman paces, where each pace represented two steps. Why a pace should represent two steps is a mystery to me but it is possible that the Romans used this explanation to define a measurement that already existed.

There are obviously 60 megalithic miles to one Minoan degree of arc. If we multiply this number by 366, we should get the circumference of the Earth. The result is 21,960 megalithic miles, which in metric terms is 40,009.8 kilometres. The modern estimation of the polar circumference of the Earth varies. Many authorities accept 40,010 km as being the definitive measurement. The estimation arrived at by multiplying 60 megalithic miles by 366, working on there being 36.6 megalithic yards to the Minoan second of arc, is at variance with accepted modern estimation by less than one kilometre. This is remarkably accurate. Moreover, it is so close to the modern figure that it is surely evidence that the Minoans did indeed regard 36.6 megalithic yards as being equal to one Minoan second of arc.

Of course, it is possible that the Minoans, or whoever devised

103

the megalithic yard, never intended to measure the circumference of the Earth at all. The fact that they managed to do so may have been a by-product of defining smaller distances. These can be established by measuring the angle from given locations on the Earth's surface to a particular point in space, for example to the celestial North Pole (this is one of the points at which the Earth's axis intersects the celestial sphere, a sphere of indeterminate size where the observer is at the centre). The difference in angles can be compared and measurements defined accordingly. However, from this starting point it would not have been difficult to establish the circumference of the Earth.

It is worth noting that on this scale ten Minoan seconds of arc are equivalent to 14,640 megalithic inches or 366 megalithic yards. Because both of these numbers are so important to the Minoan methods of calculation, the first being the number of days in a Minoan Cycle and the second representing the number of days in the Minoan year, it is possible that the Minoans may have originally adopted a system which allowed only six seconds of arc to one minute of arc and not the 60 seconds we use today.

Interestingly, then, the more modern invention of the nautical mile seems to have been an attempt to re-invent something that had been devised thousands of years previously in order to divide the Earth geometrically into units that closely fitted the geometric segments. Although evolved at radically different periods, the megalithic mile and the nautical mile are very similar: the nautical mile is slightly longer, bearing in mind the difference between a 360-degree and a 366-degree circle.

The preceding megalithic mathematical models seem to indicate that the Minoans considered the Minoan minute of arc to contain six seconds of arc rather than the 60 seconds we use today. Since I have no definite proof of this, except the way the numbers fall, I have included both possibilities in the table opposite. The essential significance of the Minoan system remains valid, irrespective of whether there are six or 60 Minoan seconds to one Minoan degree. When referring to a complete circle, I have classified this as the Minoan Circle. The use of this term merely indicates a circle (in this case, one representing an estimated circumference of the Earth) which is composed of 366 degrees, rather than the more familiar 360 degrees of our own mathematics.

Megalithic measurements and modern equivalents

Model	Geometric Measurement	Time (mean solar day)	Distance		
			Megalithic	Imperial	Metric
6"M	1"M = ⅙'M	0.6557 sec	366 myd (14,640 mgin)	996.252 ft	303.658 m
60"M	1"M = ⅟₆₀'M	0.0655 sec	36.6 myd (1,464 mgin)	99.6252 ft	30.3658 m
60"M	1'M = ⅟₆₀°M	3.9344 sec	1 mmile (2,196 myd)	1.1321 miles	1.8219 km
60"M	1°M = ⅟₃₆₆ of Earth's circumference	236.0655 sec	60 mmiles (131,760 myd)	67.9262 miles	109.3164 km
60"M	1 zodiac sign* = 1/12 of Earth's circumference	120 min (1 Mhr)	1,830 mmiles (4,018,68 myd)	2071.7513 miles	333.1522 km
60"M	1 Minoan circle = 336°M	24 hours	21,960 mmiles (48,224.16 myd)	24,861,0158 miles	40,009.839 km

* All based on the mean of 30° and 31° signs

KEY

'M	=	Minoan minute of arc
"M	=	Minoan second of arc
°M	=	Minoan degree
mgin	=	megalithic inch
Mhr	=	Minoan hour
min	=	minute in a mean solar day
mmile	=	megalithic mile
myd	=	megalithic yard
sec	=	second in a mean solar day

Leaving aside for the moment the reasons that the Minoans may have had for dividing the circumference of the Earth in this way, we are left with the inevitable conclusion that there must have been a link between the megalith builders of Western Europe and the astronomer priests of ancient Crete. Such an association may not be as unlikely as it might first appear. After all, many of the megalithic monuments were being built around the same time as the Minoan civilisation was flourishing in Crete. We know from contemporary accounts that the Cretans of the period were great seafarers. They traded extensively with Egypt and visited the areas of present-day Libya and Syria. There were Minoan outposts on many of the Greek islands, on the mainland, on Cyprus and on Sicily.

Of course, this is a far cry from asserting that the Minoans were capable of passing through the Pillars of Hercules and out into the Atlantic Ocean, even supposing that they had the incentive to try. Such a journey would have been epic by Bronze Age standards, although it is by no means out of the question. In *The White Goddess* Robert Graves asserts that parts of the British Isles and especially Ireland were peopled from the Stone Age onwards by people of what we would now call Greek stock. *The White Goddess* is a fascinating exploration of interweaving myths and legends, many of which Robert Graves claims are from a series of common European themes, and some of them are still to be found in the folklore of peoples as far apart as the west of Ireland and the furthest reaches of the Mediterranean. It is just conceivable that some of these early visitors to Britain originally came from Crete, settled in these distant lands, and brought with them a knowledge of Minoan accomplishments as well as astronomical know-how.

There is another possibility, however, and it is one that dates back to an idea that was popular a couple of decades ago. Some carvings were found on one of the giant stones that make up the sarsen circle of Stonehenge – in addition, that is, to the many attempts at immortality chiselled into the stones during the last three centuries or so. The carvings in question are of a dagger and what looks like an axe. It was considered at the time that the dagger bore a striking resemblance to those popular in the late Bronze Age in the Greek kingdom of Mycenae. Perhaps, it was suggested, the later stage of Stonehenge, at least, was masterminded by

Mycenaean engineers and was not entirely of local origin. The idea did not really stick for very long, however. Around the same time, revisions were being made concerning the age of Stonehenge III, that part of the monument on which the carvings were discovered. It seems that this portion of the circle was erected around 2000 BC, some 400 years before the Mycenaean civilisation. The Mycenaeans, therefore, could not have been involved in the building of Stonehenge III. In any case, the experts said, the carvings were very weathered and could easily be meant to represent weapons of local origin.

One fact that the experts in this field seem to have overlooked, however, is the close connections between the Minoan civilisation and that of the Mycenaeans. After the fall of the Minoan civilisation on Crete around 1450 BC, the island was ruled by Mycenae; a strong cross-fertilisation had existed between the two cultures for some time before this. Stonehenge III was certainly not built by the Mycenaeans but it could have owed something to the Minoans. There is evidence on the ground, or rather beneath it, to show that Minoan influence in the furthest extremities of Western Europe may have been more than the passing visit of some lost or particularly adventurous Minoan sea captain. The archaeological record tends to substantiate the theory that trade existed between Britain and the Mediterranean world and particularly between the so-called Wessex Culture which was flourishing in the south of England at the time that Stonehenge III was constructed.

Many of the goods dating from a period after 2000 BC that have been found in graves in the area can be attributed to an Aegean style and are still most commonly classified as being of Mycenaean origin. Among the artefacts in question is a beautiful gold cup from Rillaton and three gold earrings found at Normanton near Stonehenge which are almost certainly of Minoan manufacture. Faience beads (earthenware beads that have been decorated and glazed) which were known to have been made in Crete or exported there from Egypt and a number of weapons including double axes have also been found. In addition, there is amber, of which the Wessex folk were especially fond, other gold artefacts and a strange bowl which was found further to the north and west in Caergwrie in Clwyd, Wales. This bowl seems to be in the shape of a ship. It is of exquisite quality with much gold ornamentation and carries

A late Minoan amphora with a stunning representation of an octopus.

'eyes' of the type still painted on to the prows of Greek ships. No exact date can be offered for the bowl and though many authorities place it well after the Minoan period it does seem to indicate the possibility of visitors from far to the south and east.

Confusion over finds that are claimed to be Mycenaean, when in reality they could just as easily be Minoan, is quite understandable. Even before the sudden end of the Minoan civilisation on Crete, there seems to have been a brisk trade or even a dynastic connection between the two cultures. Minoan influence shows itself early in Mycenaean art and architecture. After Knossos, and presumably the rest of Crete, fell under the domination of the Mycenaeans some time around 1450 BC, these influences become even stronger. Although the Mycenaeans were lovers of gold and ornamentation, they were essentially a martial race and lacked the fineness of touch that was second nature to the Minoan artists. It is also a fact that some of the greatest architectural achievements of the Mycenaeans came after their conquest of the Minoans, and here may lie part of the evidence for a Minoan influence in the building of Stonehenge III.

Much has been written about Stonehenge. It was a long-term project by any stretch of the imagination and its construction spanned the rise and decline of a number of cultures in the area. Different builders had different ideas concerning what the monument should look like and, more to the point, what it should be used for. It is now almost universally accepted that most stone circles have an astronomical function. Back in early neolithic times, this site on Salisbury Plain already contained a fairly simple stone circle, the function of which was probably to track the passage of the Sun and the Moon, as well as assisting in the prediction of eclipses.

Stonehenge III was the culmination of successive attempts to refine the structure. Probably around 2150 BC, stones of immense size were brought from 321 kilometres (200 miles) away, though this stage of the monument was never completed in the way the engineers had probably intended. Instead, the now famous circle of sarsen stones was quarried from the local Marlborough Downs, some 24 kilometres (15 miles) to the north. There were 40 uprights connected by 35 lintels which together create the impressive circle, and five free-standing trilithons (a trilithon consists of two uprights and a lintel).

The degree of expertise required to move and erect these massive stones was extremely sophisticated. The lintels were not simply placed on top of the uprights, as might have been expected, but instead the stones were locked together with mortise and tenon joints, more reminiscent of woodworking techniques than stoneworking skills. It had probably been the intention of the builders at this time to erect the previously discarded blue stones in a spiral outside the sarsens, since there are abandoned holes on the site that show this spiral. Instead, they ended up as another circle and horseshoe within the great sarsen monument, as can be seen on the site today.

Leaving aside exactly what the monument was meant to do in astronomical terms, there are some interesting speculations concerning this phase of Stonehenge which, it could be argued, show a distinct Minoan influence. For example, the use of

40 uprights in the sarsen arrangement again echoes the Minoan fascination with that number. The intended spiral outside the giant arrangement might also have Cretan overtones, since the Minoans were obsessed with spiral designs. Most interesting of all is the fact that the final phase of the monument, known as Stonehenge IIIa, has been dated at about 2100 BC, although the abandoned spiral is later, from around 1490 BC. The abandoning of the spiral in about 1490 BC is very significant, however, for it is almost exactly the time when Minoan supremacy in the Mediterranean gave way to Mycenae.

Although it is known that the Minoan civilisation came to what appears to have been an abrupt end, the cause of its demise is far from certain. It is equally well known that when the Minoan civilisation ended, the Mycenaeans took over. Some authorities consider that civil insurrection on Crete allowed the foreigners to gain a foothold on the island, while others conjecture that a huge volcanic eruption on the nearby island of Santorini which occurred at about that time could have created tidal waves that destroyed the Minoan navy and earthquakes that wrecked the palaces and perhaps the very infrastructure of Minoan society. It is known that fire destroyed many of the towns and cities some time around 1450 BC, the origin of which could have been the eruption of Santorini.

The martial aspect of Minoan life, so conspicuous by its absence prior to this period, now became prominent as evidenced by grave findings and other artefacts, indicating how much influence the warlike Mycenaeans were exerting. The palaces at Malia, Phaistos and also possibly Zakro were abandoned. The island appears to have been ruled from Knossos, which, although never again achieving its former glory, was still inhabited after 1450 BC. The trade-off did not turn out to be entirely one-sided, however. Minoan craftsmen went to the mainland where their influence on the art and architecture of the Mycenaean culture was almost immediately apparent.

Mycenae became great during this period and began to create huge citadels with massive fortifications. Perhaps the greatest of them all is the citadel of Mycenae itself. Even classical scholars remarked on the massive proportions of this edifice, with its defensive walls averaging 15 feet in thickness. The early Greek visitors called these fortifications Cyclopedian, for they considered that only the one-eyed giants of their mythology, the Cyclops, could have had the strength to build such mighty structures. The technology to do so probably came from Crete, for Mycenae was built around 1300 BC, after the annexation of Crete by the Mycenaean empire. The Lion Gate was also found on this site, a structure very reminiscent of the giant trilithons of Stonehenge. As part of its adornment, the Lion Gate carries a central pillar in a frieze above the entrance. This has been suggested as typical of Minoan influence on the site, the pillar being such an important part of Minoan building and religion. Stonemasons' marks known to have been used extensively on Crete have also been found on Mycenaean sites, which adds further weight to the supposition that Cretan workers were busy on the mainland.

Stonemasons and engineers who could cut, dress and move the vast quantities of stone necessary to build the huge palace at Knossos and who would later be called upon to erect the citadels to keep Mycenae's enemies at bay, would not have found the sarsen circle at Stonehenge to be too great a challenge. Why they would want to undertake the enterprise is uncertain, however. Perhaps there was some sort of confederacy between Minoan Crete and these strange, weather-beaten lands far to the north and west. It might not be too fanciful to suggest that, although Stonehenge III had served more than a ritual purpose, the Minoan visitors simply wanted to put their own seal on what was undoubtedly an already impressive structure.

Goods from graves associated with the period of Stonehenge III show the Wessex people to have been great traders and perhaps even travellers in their own right. They were certainly wealthy and had access to raw materials, such as tin from Cornwall, not readily available in Crete. It is even possible that Minoan engineers were in some way employed to assist in the work on the site, leaving their mark in religious and architectural terms, albeit in an altered form once the Mycenaeans rose to power and the blue stone spiral was then abandoned in favour of the inner circle that can still be clearly seen today.

The inhabitants of what is now Britain had no written language of their own at that time. What we know of them comes to us via myths and legends, together with the limited archaeological record. On Crete, the language and culture of the Minoans was being changed to suit the new times brought about by the rule of Mycenae. Forms of writing were altered. Hieroglyphs, if they were ever intended to be writing in the strict sense of the word, gave way to the linear scripts, some of which have now been deciphered. The deciphered texts tend to deal with the practicalities of life: the number of slaves owned by the king, business transactions, and inventories of various kinds. They do not relate to events that took place before the fall of the Minoan civilisation. If the Minoans ever did play a part in the building of megalithic structures in the British Isles, written accounts of the events may never come to light in Crete and certainly not in Britain. The only other evidence for Minoan involvement in the building of the megaliths is to be found on the sites themselves, in the mathematical precision of the placing of the stones and among the archaeological remains to be found in the attendant graves.

Fanciful theories have been put forward in the past about the building of Stonehenge, one author even suggesting that the Egyptians had played a part in its construction. If this had been the case, they seem to have been very careful to leave no evidence of their presence on the site, though the same is not true in the case of the Minoans who left a mark on the culture of southern England. Archaeological finds can never show a complete record of life in any period and the fact that goods of an Aegean origin have been found in rather significant quantity may indicate that what has come to light is only a small part of what had been brought to Britain by the Minoans. Much more may yet be found and still lies beneath the chalky earth, waiting to be discovered by a future archaeologist or diligent searcher.

A generally accepted theory concerning the earlier stages of Stonehenge is that the monument was built, in part at least, to predict lunar eclipses. Myths concerning Stonehenge as it presently stands mostly attest to the monument being created as a temple to Apollo who was a solar god. Professor Fred Hoyle considers that only in the first two phases of Stonehenge is there any real evidence that meaningful, astronomical observations were being made, and he believes that the latter phase of the monument shows little astronomical significance. Other authorities disagree, most especially Professor Gerald Hawkins who in his book *Stonehenge*

*The sun setting over the ruins of Stonehenge on
Salisbury Plain in southern England.*

Decoded claims to have found many alignments associated with the
sarsen circle that could have meant that observations were still being
undertaken on the site as late as 1500 BC.

Perhaps the Minoans' assistance in the project brought a
greater mathematical significance to Stonehenge and they may well
have left a legacy of their own calendar system in the arrangement
of 40 upright sarsen stones. More work on the geometry of the
circle is necessary and perhaps on others in the locality to establish
whether the 366-degree circle favoured by the Minoans forms any
part of the working matrix of Stonehenge III. As for the dagger
carved on the sarsen, the Mediterranean looks of which first
suggested the possibility of a Greek connection with the
monument, there is a statue in Heraklion museum that depicts a
man carrying a dagger at his belt. The weapon is not unlike that in
the carving on the sarsen stone at Stonehenge, particularly with
regard to the large, round pommel which is in evidence in both
weapons. The carving of a dagger at Stonehenge is not easy to
photograph, however, and is only really visible under certain
lighting conditions.

We know from Professor Thom's evidence, and from datings
associated with sites all over Britain and in parts of France, that the

113

megalithic yard was in use many centuries before the rise of Minoan Crete. This would indicate that there was a definite cultural connection between the people inhabiting Britain from the late Stone Age onward and the people living in Crete. Perhaps the tales of early visitors to Britain from the eastern Mediterranean, so forcefully argued by Robert Graves in *The White Goddess*, are not fanciful at all. There is a distinct possibility that early thinkers and builders in what is now Britain were affected by an as yet unknown culture which also played a part in the rise of civilisation in Crete. Megalithic cultures are known to have flourished on the islands of the Mediterranean, for example, in Malta.

Crete stands along a line that is 35 degrees north of the equator. Many miles to the west and beyond the Pillars of Hercules, the mountain tops of an oceanic range rise out of the Atlantic to form the islands that are now known as the Azores. They are close to the same latitude as Crete, being 38 degrees north of the equator. It is to this location that many writers have looked to find the legendary Atlantis described in some detail by Plato. Geologists are presently of the opinion that no sizeable land mass has ever existed in this location. However, if it had and was destroyed by volcanoes and earthquakes as Plato's work indicates, the survivors of the catastrophe could well have made landfalls down the western coasts of Britain or found their way into the Mediterranean, probably following trade routes that were already known to them.

Some archaeologists speculate that the original theory of a megalithic culture that started in the far east of Europe and spread westward is the reverse of what the evidence on the ground actually shows. In other words, those early inhabitants of the British Isles may have been among the first megalithic peoples, the influence then gradually moving east. Is it possible that the origin of this tendency to build large monuments which often seem to have astronomical connections lies far to the west beneath the deep waters of the Atlantic Ocean, despite the present views of geologists? If present geological thinking is to be believed, the answer would have to be 'No', although the ancient origins of the megalithic yard and the precise way it fits into the Earth's circumference still cannot be ignored. When we take into consideration the period of history we are dealing with, we realise that this is mathematics of an extremely high calibre. There is no known candidate in the right geographical location for its inception several thousand years before the birth of the Minoan civilisation.

CHAPTER TWELVE

PLOTTING A COURSE – EARLY NAVIGATION

The Phaistos Disc was capable of great accuracy when it came to plotting the Sun or the ascendant (the sign that is rising above the eastern horizon) at any particular time. Outside celestial navigation, there is no reason to develop a system with the level of accuracy inherent in the Minoan system. Of course, one reason for attempting to achieve an objective is because it represents a challenge. Presumably this was as true in Minoan Crete as it is in our own age. However, it seems highly unlikely that the level of accuracy inherent in the Minoan system was achieved merely because someone responded to a challenge. There must have been a practical purpose behind the accuracy. Legend tells us that these remarkable people not only invented weights and measures and discs but that they also built lighthouses. There can be only one reason for lighthouses – to illuminate hazardous areas at sea for ships sailing at night. The evidence that remains after several thousand years points to the fact that the Minoans may not have been merely the land-hugging sailors who only ventured out to sea in daylight that these Bronze Age people are presently supposed to have been.

Mankind is an inherently curious species. One aspect of our insatiable curiosity that has dominated our endeavours for thousands of years is our desire to know what is round the next corner. This need to know what lies beyond the next hill, round every new bend in the river or across that narrow stretch of sea has driven us to explore the world from very early in our history. There is no reason to suppose that the Minoans were any different. They,

**The Dolphin Fresco from the palace at Knossos
testifies to the Minoans' knowledge of the sea.**

too, must have wanted to know what was beyond their island home. They, too must have had the urge to explore beyond the immediate horizons of Crete. The island was capable of supplying everything that its early settlers could possibly have needed but it was not rich in metal ores. This deficiency alone may have been enough of a spur to the Minoans for them to venture forth to find out what lay over the horizon. The Minoans would not have needed to sail very far from Crete merely to fish. Even allowing for the fact that seafood undoubtedly supplemented the diet of the early Cretans, as it supplements the diet of the inhabitants of the island today, this would require only relatively short journeys by sea and certainly would not necessitate the crossing of vast stretches of water.

However, it would appear that the Minoans may well have undertaken such voyages as a matter of course. Is there any evidence to support the idea that they sailed the seas beyond sight of land in search of the unknown? It seems that there is compelling evidence to support this theory. To enable the Minoans to have sailed beyond sight of land and into the unknown, they would have had to have possessed a means of keeping track of where they were. And this would have meant being able to determine how far they had travelled. What the Minoan sailors needed was a reliable method of determining where their craft was in relation to their home port and other known locations at any particular point in time. Since the connection between the Minoan second of arc and the megalithic yard suggests that the Minoans knew the precise dimensions of the Earth, it seems likely that they also used this knowledge for navigational purposes.

Sailing in Bronze Age times was very dangerous. Aside from the possibility of coming ashore somewhere unfamiliar to find yourself surrounded by a hostile populace, the Mediterranean is no millpond. The wrecking of ships due to storms at sea must have been an all-too-common event in ancient times. Most sea journeys in these remote times are generally accepted to have taken place in daylight hours and wherever possible within direct sight of land so as to minimise the dangers. The position of the Sun throughout the day would offer a rudimentary clue to direction, as would the stars at night. However, night sailings were inherently more dangerous simply because you could not see where you were going. If the helmsman had no knowledge of obstructions like submerged rocks and did not know his position, a night sailing could be fraught with peril.

There have always been skilled navigators, even among those primitive civilisations who took to the seas. The Polynesians, for example, appear to have travelled across vast areas of ocean in the Pacific. It is known that they sailed by night as well as during the day and that they had named and knew the positions of many of the fixed stars. They could steer by means of half a coconut filled with water in which the helmsman watched the reflection of a particular star. By keeping the reflection in the coconut water, the helmsman had some idea of the direction his craft was taking. A similar form of navigation may also have been used in European waters in early times, though this must always have been a risky business in the relatively cramped European seaways compared to the open waters of the Pacific – there are a lot more obstacles in the Mediterranean than in the great expanse of the Pacific and in a much smaller area.

It is the opinion of Professor Roy of the University of Glasgow that the origin of the zodiac constellations, which he attributed to the Minoan civilisation, was almost certainly associated with their search for ever-better forms of navigation. He based this theory on the fact that those constellations that are not circumpolar must always rise and set at points that form definite angles with the east and west for a fixed latitude. This knowledge can be used to provide compass bearings throughout the night and would have been a definite boon to these early mariners. He showed that this aid to navigation was still being used in the twentieth century by the inhabitants of the Caroline Islands of the south-west Pacific, north of Papua New Guinea.

It is my contention, based on the numbering system employed on the Phaistos Disc, together with the legends connecting the Minoans with measurements and lighthouses, that the Minoans took things considerably further than this and established a system of navigation that would not be bettered until medieval times.

We have already seen that it would have been possible for the Minoans to divide the surface of the Earth into units with reference to the sky that was passing overhead. One Minoan second of arc of the heavens represented something like 100 standard feet, while one Minoan minute of arc could be judged as being very close to the modern mile. This would allow a system of grids to be placed across that area of the Earth known to the Minoans, similar to that used on modern maps. This would have formed a very accurate system of measuring longitude and latitude. Of course, the Minoans had not circumnavigated the globe, though by implication they must surely have surmised that the world is round and known its dimensions.

As long as some sort of reasonably accurate chart is available, and provided that there is a good measuring system with which to superimpose a usable grid on to that chart, it is not difficult to ascertain your location at sea, even though the vessel may be many miles from land. Modern navigation relies more and more on satellites which can determine the position of a vessel to within a few metres. Prior to this, however, the most useful instrument to the navigator was the sextant. This is an optical instrument which allows any observer to calculate the angular distance between, say, the Sun and the horizon. It can also be used with a reference point on the horizon: for example, a distant tower of known height. In the case of solar sightings, there is an almanac produced each year to which the navigator can refer in order to establish the geographical position of the Sun and known fixed stars. With the angular measurements obtained from the sextant, the correct use of the almanac and an accurate knowledge of the time at a fixed point, such as Greenwich, it is possible to make an accurate assessment of the position of a ship at sea. Before the eighteenth century and the invention of the chronometer, however, there was no precise way of determining the time at any place on the Earth's surface other than where the mariner was. Local time is all very well but it does not help with navigation.

However, ingenious ways were used to overcome this problem. The most important of these was known as dead reckoning. If a line, marked out by knots at regular intervals of known length, is paid out from the stern of a boat, it is possible to ascertain the speed of the craft. Repeating this procedure over a period of time, assessed perhaps by the Sun's movement, it is possible to work out how far a craft has travelled. There are many variables here, such as tide flow, and the method only works in the hands of skilled seamen aware from long years of experience what sort of compensations to make. And this method of checking the position is only effective for reasonably short distances, since it follows that inherent discrepancies are bound to multiply over a period of time so that eventually the craft may be many miles from its estimated position. However, when within sight of known reference points on land, such as lighthouses, for example, it is possible to correct the errors and establish the correct position of the craft.

This may well have been the system utilised by the ancient Minoans, for the majority of their travels took them east and west within the Mediterranean, in among the islands to the south of Greece, or south towards the African coast. Although some of the journeys would have meant being out of sight of land for some time, it would have been possible to be within sight of at least some reference points fairly often. Natural sighting points, known to be at specific distances from Crete, would have been necessary. Where these did not exist, however, the inhabitants of the many settlements that the Minoans established along the northern shores of the Mediterranean and among the Greek islands could well have erected tall towers that carried lights at night to give the Minoan navigators an accurate fix on their position.

Prior to the use of the sextant, other instruments such as astrolabes and cross-staffs were used to fulfil more or less the same job, though being more primitive in design, these were not so accurate. It is not beyond the realms of possibility that the Minoans invented some such device in order to measure the angular positions of heavenly bodies relative to the horizon. When checked against the estimated distance from their own port derived by dead reckoning, the knowledge of the position of the Sun and other heavenly bodies, which could have been established from the Phaistos Disc or more likely perhaps a close cousin dedicated to the task, would have offered a reasonably accurate estimation as to the position of the vessel.

If this sounds a little far-fetched, it should be remembered that the seasoned mariner in Minoan times also had a number of other weapons in his armoury. He knew about the North Pole, for example. There was, in fact, no clear pole star in Minoan times, though the Minoans could have probably worked out where the celestial North Pole was from the square of Ursa Minor. This should have given the Minoan navigator at least one good fixed point to steer by, even aside from the angles formed east and west by the zodiac constellations. In most cases, he would also have known the seaways that he plied reasonably well from memory, together with seasonal variations of tides and currents in various locations. Another singular advantage was the fact that he was usually travelling within a fairly confined band north and south. It might be an over-simplification but it is nevertheless reasonable to suggest that if you travel far enough north in the Mediterranean, you are certain to happen upon the coast of Europe, while if you venture south you will sooner or later hit the coast of Africa.

Just how far the Minoans took their mathematics in terms of seamanship is very hard to determine. They appear to have had at their disposal all the requirements of a very advanced system, except for an accurate means of measuring time relative to a known fixed point. Using the astronomical data and mathematics that they were familiar with, it would have been possible for them to judge local time, day or night, with quite staggering accuracy, though this is still not the same as being able to keep pace with a sundial or water clock that might be hundreds of miles away from the ship.

However, even without recourse to the chronometer, which revolutionised navigation and made transglobal journeys much safer, the ancient Minoans did have much of the information that they needed in order to undertake the more limited journeys that they undoubtedly took, even extending far to the west, taking in perhaps the British Isles and the Atlantic coast of Western Europe.

But perhaps that most elusive requirement for successful navigation, a knowledge of absolute time, was not beyond the scope of Minoan mariners either.

CHAPTER THIRTEEN

MEASUREMENTS

From the very start of my quest to show exactly what the Phaistos Disc was and what it might imply about the long-dead civilisation that created it, I was always aware that this one artefact may not be enough on its own to substantiate my faith in Minoan mathematical skills. So many of the hypotheses rest on each other like bricks in a wall, and it could be argued that if any one of them were shown to be suspect, the whole edifice might come tumbling down. Science, quite rightly, demands proof and although the weight of evidence would tend to suggest that my ideas were sound, some independent verification was always going to be a distinct advantage.

The close association between the Minoan system and the megalithic yard was, in itself, a solid enough prop and yet even the meticulous Professor Alexander Thom has his detractors. So it was with great relief, though rather late in my investigations, that I came across a piece of independent evidence that seems to support my claims about the Minoans. Not only does this fairly recently discovered information support my belief that the Minoans used a 366-degree circle but it may also show that Professor Thom's megalithic inch and megalithic yard are both realities. The reason that the true worth of this evidence has never been realised lies only in the fact that no understanding of Minoan mathematics has been established before now.

Back in the 1960s, an architect and stonemason by the name of Professor J. Walter Graham very carefully measured the palaces at Phaistos, Malia and Knossos. He then made comparisons between the measurements and eventually came across a common unit, measuring 30.36 centimetres, which he christened the Minoan foot. His findings were verified in the major buildings of all three palaces which, although different in size, seemed to have been constructed using a common measurement that must have been in use throughout the island. This unit, Professor Graham asserted, was clearly common to all the palaces; it could be shown that all the central courtyards and many of the buildings surrounding them had been built in multiples of the Minoan foot. He found, for example, that the courtyards of Malia and Phaistos both measured 170 by 80 Minoan feet.

There was always the possibility that Professor Graham was mistaken since he could have found something that did not in reality exist; it could have been mere coincidence that the measurements seemed to fit the Minoan foot theory. However, the crunch came with the subsequent discovery of the previously unknown palace of Zakro on the eastern coast of Crete. This palace, it was soon observed, conformed to the pattern so well that nobody could now be in doubt as to the validity of the Minoan foot.

At first sight, the existence of this measurement appeared to do little to substantiate my own theories, mainly because the Minoan foot is not a 'sensible' or logical division of the megalithic yard. However, the connection was there and I soon found it. The Minoan second of arc, according to my theory, when seen as a part of the Earth's circumference, measures 36.6 megalithic yards which is 1,464 megalithic inches. In modern terms, this is 30.3657 metres (99.63 feet). Professor Graham's proposed Minoan foot, which is equivalent to 30.36 centimetres, divides into this 100 times, with an error of only 0.57 centimetres. This seems to be incontrovertible proof of the existence of the Minoan second of arc.

If my earlier assumption that there were only six Minoan seconds to the Minoan minute is correct, then one Minoan second of arc, as measured on the ground, is 366 megalithic yards or 14,640 megalithic inches. Both of these numbers have already been shown to be very significant in Minoan terms since they form an integral part of Minoan geometry and the Minoan calendar cycles. This same distance is almost 1,000 Minoan feet (the discrepancy is equivalent to about five centimetres). The number of megalithic inches in 1,000 Minoan feet turns out to be a very interesting number indeed, namely 14,637.22251. This is, for all practical purposes, the very same number as that derived from multiplying together the numbers of symbols on side A and side B of the Phaistos Disc: 119 times 123 is 14,637.

It is hard to believe that the derivation of this number is a chance event. It seems to have been deliberately engineered into the system. Why the Minoans evolved the system of domestic measurements shown here may never be known, although building structures the size of palaces without a reliable system of measurement would have been rather difficult. However, since the megalithic yard and presumably, therefore, the megalithic mile were both in use across much of Europe prior to the rise of the Minoans, it is possible that the later Minoan foot was adopted for ease of use in the construction of buildings on Crete. The Minoan foot is so close to its modern counterpart, being about $11^{15}/_{16}$ inches in length, that the Minoan foot may have survived to this day; the Minoan foot and its modern counterpart could almost be one and the same. No megalithic equivalent seems to have existed, although why the Minoans did not simply divide the megalithic yard into three for smaller measurements is something of a mystery. A possible answer to this puzzle could be that because the megalithic yard contained 40 megalithic inches it could not be easily divided into three equal sections. To divide it into four would have been much easier but this may have provided a unit that was too small for practical use.

What is clear, despite the many mysteries that still surround the measuring system used in the palaces on Crete, is that there is a very close relationship between this system and that associated with the megalithic monuments. Surely this was not chance. A gradual advancement in Minoan measuring techniques does not account for this, for the circumference of the Earth, derived by the divisions allowed by the Minoan foot, comes out at 40,002 kilometres which is certainly very close to the modern estimation of 40,010 kilometres; using megalithic yards the result is somewhat more accurate at 40,009 kilometres. Nevertheless, both are astonishingly close to the modern figure and both remain valid as natural consequences of there being 60 Minoan seconds of arc to one Minoan minute of arc and 60 Minoan minutes to one Minoan degree with 366 Minoan degrees to the Minoan circle.

Without an understanding of the Minoan 366-degree circle, which itself originates from the Minoan calendar, neither the megalithic yard nor the Minoan foot appear to be anything but arbitrary as units of length. An understanding of the Minoan 366-degree circle means that both become logical units of length, deliberate divisions of the Earth's circumference.

Did Professor Graham's Minoan foot exist before the rise of Minoan Crete? In order to find out, it seems that the megalithic monuments of Western Europe, particularly the standing stone circles and other monuments so carefully studied by Professor Thom, will have to be looked at and measured again. It is, of course, possible that Minoan engineers ultimately found the megalithic yard cumbersome to work with and decided to invent what is, in effect, a more user-friendly system for their domestic architecture. In fact, in terms of subdividing the Earth's circumference to a very high degree of accuracy (based on the Minoan 366-degree circle) the two systems, i.e. the Minoan foot and the megalithic yard, are equally valid.

CHAPTER FOURTEEN

THE NUMBER 40

One of the greatest puzzles that emerged in my researches was why the Minoans had chosen to base their number system on the number 40 rather than on any other number. Clearly, the number 40 had some significance otherwise the Minoans would not have chosen to use it. But what was it?

Of course, if a calendar is based on a 366-day year and has to be reconciled with the solar year of just over 365 days, the number 40 is particularly useful, because it is at the end of 40 years that the 366-day year and the solar year differ by one Minoan month of 30.5 days. The Minoan Cycle of 40 years may have been established as a result of an awareness of this. It may have been enough to give the number 40 a magical significance to the Minoans. And yet there had to be more to it than this. Perhaps the number 40 held a particular significance before the invention of the Minoan calendar and for this reason the Minoans incorporated it in their system.

Fertility was of supreme importance to Minoan beliefs as, indeed, it was to most early cultures. Fertility was represented by a goddess and she was probably one of the earliest deities to be worshipped because fertility represented life and its continuation. Despite the fact that she was later demoted in the order of importance, her significance to early peoples is obvious because of the wide variety of her forms throughout the world. One factor that is of particular significance with regard to these early representations of the goddess is that she is invariably depicted as being pregnant. Undoubtedly there was symbolism here, for the pregnant goddess was representative of the forces of nature and their cyclical change with the seasons. In other words, the birth–death–rebirth cycle. It is possible that the pregnant goddess also brought to mind the number 40 because this is approximately the number of weeks in the human gestation period.

The seven-day period, which we now refer to as the week, may well have been one of the earliest and most easily definable yardsticks which mankind used in recognition of the cosmic cycles. The reason for this lies in the fact that seven days is on average a quarter of the full lunar cycle which is just in excess of 28 days long. The cycle is divided into equal parts, new moon to first quarter, first quarter to full moon, full moon to last quarter, and last quarter to new moon again; seven days represents the nearest whole number for each period.

It has been shown that the basis of all timekeeping, geometry and astronomy lies in the number systems that were employed by the Minoans, which are inferred from the Phaistos Disc. The association of minutes and seconds with time and angular measurement has been lost and yet there is a very real connection when the mathematics of the solar system is looked at from a Minoan standpoint. But if the number 40 was so very important to the whole system, why is it no longer with us as a usable unit and why is it not mentioned in ancient writings? In fact, as far as the latter is concerned, there are many references to the number 40. For example, there are numerous examples in both the Old and New Testaments and these always relate in some way to periods of time.

The first reference to the number 40 in the Old Testament is probably in Exodus. According to Exodus, the Israelites spent 40 years in the desert after fleeing from Egypt before reaching the Promised Land. Repeatedly the number 40 shows itself as having a religious as well as calendrical significance. A period of 40 days, the microcosm of the 40-year period, also crops up on a significant number of occasions. In the Book of Kings, for example, we are told that the prophet Elijah was fortified by a wondrous food given to him by an angel prior to a pilgrimage that was to endure 40 days. The New Testament Gospels relate that Christ spent 40 days in the wilderness during which he was tempted by Satan, prior to his baptism by John the Baptist and the start of his mission on Earth. The period between Easter and Christ's Ascension is celebrated as 40 days, while Lent also lasts for 40 days.

Such periods of time could be taken literally to mean precisely what is stated but it appears more likely that they are symbolic. Whichever is the case, they imply an understanding of a unit of measurement that may well have been known for a very long time and which originated in Minoan Crete. In the not so distant past, we find another reference to the 40-day period in the word 'quarantine' which is derived from the Italian *quarantina* which means 40 days – the length of time that a ship suspected of carrying an infectious disease such as plague had to ride at anchor in isolation before it was considered safe to be approached. Why 40 days was the required span is questionable, since this bears no relation to the incubation period of any disease, although it should be borne in mind that when the quarantine was introduced no one knew that.

Natural numbers, such as those derived from solar or lunar observations, are understandable so it is not surprising that 7, 28, 30 and 365 tend to crop up time and again as significant numbers in history. The number 40 is a rather different kettle of fish, however, and at first sight does not appear to relate to either solar or lunar activity. But we should not forget the relationship between 40 Earth years, 65 orbits of Venus and 166 orbits of Mercury which the Minoans seem to have understood and which could have formed part of the logic behind the creation of the 40-year Minoan Cycle in the first place.

The repeated use of the number 40 in writings, which in some cases are from sources as old as the Minoan civilisation, would indicate that the number 40 did have a great significance to Bronze Age peoples, especially in a calendrical sense. It is my contention that the use of the number 40 was part of a megalithic numerical system which may have been invented in Crete and that its significance was known far and wide. As with all the other components of the Minoan form of seeing time, space and distance, the significance of the number 40 eventually became no more than a race memory once the system had fallen into disuse. And it is also probable that our Bronze Age ancestors also considered 40 years to be an average life expectancy.

CHAPTER FIFTEEN

MYTHS AND LEGENDS

The chances of an artefact such as the Phaistos Disc escaping the ravages of time are extremely small, so perhaps we should not be too surprised that no similar examples have been found so far – notwithstanding George's belief that others had been found and spirited away from the island never to be seen again outside some hidden private collection. There is always the possibility that other discs may be discovered in the future, for there are almost certainly rich archaeological veins on Crete that have not yet been tapped. In the meantime, we have only this one small link with a system of mathematics and astronomy, both of which are precursors of our own modern versions, though in some ways the old and the new are very different.

As I undertook the background research for this book, I became more and more convinced that Minoan Crete was a super-civilisation, originating in a period when only the kingdom of Egypt could rival it for learning or importance. In the case of the Egyptians, who were meticulous in these matters, we have a wealth of written material that can attest to their science and their religion as well as their daily lives. The Minoans were more enigmatic, for although it is possible to walk among the ruins of their palaces to be impressed by the architectural accomplishments of this long-dead race, there is little beyond such ruins to place these people in any historical context with regard to their intellectual accomplishments.

Ironically, considering that Crete now forms part of Greece, it seems to have been the ancient Greeks who did the most to eclipse

Minoan accomplishments in science, mainly by digesting them, later to regurgitate them in the guise of original thought. This may be rather uncharitable, however, since many hundreds of years separated Minoan Crete and the greatest of the classical scholars. The Mycenaeans, who had so successfully assimilated Crete into their own culture, made great use of those skills of Minoan engineers that suited their martial needs and they went some way towards achieving a richer artistic form than had formerly existed. What they may have failed to do, however, is to retain certain aspects of Minoan religion in the original form, a religion which doubtless encapsulated the wealth of astronomical and mathematical knowledge that appears to have been so carefully nurtured in Minoan Crete.

The rise of the power of Greece with its many kingdoms and city states allowed its men of learning to amass knowledge from the four corners of the known world. It would seem that much of what they discovered was of Minoan origin, so that many aspects of Minoan thought came to Greece via a fairly tortuous route. Synthesised through the mainstream of Greek culture and heritage, these ideas and discoveries have been affecting the western world ever since. Few now doubt that classical Greece owed much to Minoan Crete, many of whose deities first found form among the mountains and plains of that lovely island. Even the Greeks themselves, anxious to preserve the local origins of their own religious practices, knew that Zeus, father of all their gods and goddesses, had been born and raised on Crete and had been kept safe from his father, Cronos, in a cave high up in the Dikte Mountains where he was suckled by a she-goat.

Greece also owed to Crete many of the embodiments of the feminine godhead, not least of all Athene herself. Although subjugated by a more patriarchal society than that which had flourished in the days of Minos, the goddess was still important to the classical Greeks. She was found in a multitude of forms among the temples that were built on many a lovely hilltop or stood in the concourses of almost every city of ancient Greece.

To many historians, this is an important Minoan legacy. Until the uncovering of the great Minoan palaces this century, even this aspect of Minoan immortality was virtually unknown, however. Again, ironically, it may be within the myths and legends so beloved of the mainland Greeks themselves that we might find some more tangible clue to the accomplishments of the Minoans, even if we have to sift and delve through them in order to recognise the true worth of what lies before our eyes. And since the shifting sands of time have totally eradicated most other aspects of Minoan astronomical accomplishments, this rich preserve of folklore, tradition and history is surely worth a second look.

For many years, the content of myths was considered by historians to be of no real worth when seeking to establish actual events in the cultures of pre-literate peoples. This point of view is quite understandable, since in the telling of these stories, that may once have been accounts of actual happenings, they have become fictionalised and distorted beyond all recognition. But to ignore everything that they have to tell us is too extreme, too short-sighted. There are some stories, especially in Greek mythology, that could carry meanings which even the later chroniclers could never have realised. Fortunately, most scholars are now more ready to accept that story-cycles can sometimes provide important evidence about past cultures. Part of the reason for this is due to the exploits of a German by the name of Heinrich Schliemann. Born into a fairly humble background in nineteenth-century Germany, Heinrich Schliemann possessed a fertile imagination and developed a love of Greek mythology. In particular, he was struck by the writer Homer, and the young Heinrich was especially fond of the *Iliad*, which tells the story of the Trojan War in graphic detail.

Because the tale is rich in mythology and deals as much with the intrigues of the gods as it does with the events on Earth, historians had generally considered the *Iliad* to be nothing more than an elaborate story, invented by an ingenious mind and penned only for its entertainment value. Schliemann saw something more in the *Iliad* and was determined to prove that Troy had really existed. As a young man, he worked diligently and eventually amassed a large enough fortune to indulge his interest in the history of Greece. After many years of painstaking and fruitless searching, he eventually happened upon an area of what is now modern Turkey, called Hiserlik. There, under a huge mound that had been known about but untouched for centuries, Heinrich Schliemann found, not one, but several Troys.

It was eventually proved beyond doubt that this was indeed

An engraving from Schliemann's **Troy and its
Ruins** *showing workmen digging in the temple
of Athena through the mound of Hiserlik.*

the location of the epic struggle to free the beautiful Helen; the
Siege of Troy had really taken place. No doubt, the political reasons
for the Trojan War were far more complex than an argument over a
queen, no matter how fair of face she may have been. Troy yielded
to Schliemann fabulous treasures and although he was not an
archaeologist in the modern sense and may have caused
considerable damage to the site during his excavations, he did at
least start people thinking again about the possibility of story-cycles
and what they might have to tell us about the lives of ancient
peoples.

Strangely enough, this same man very nearly discovered the
palace of Knossos in Crete as well. Early this century, he
endeavoured to buy the mound upon which the palace ruins stand.
Fortunately perhaps, he could not come to equitable terms with
the local owner of the place and it eventually fell to Sir Arthur
Evans, a very much more painstaking sifter of earth, to lift the ruins
from beneath their ancient mound.

My search for the truths hidden in the mythology of ancient
Greece had never been intended to lead to the discovery of vast
caches of treasure, at least, not in the accepted sense. There is a
greater treasure than gold and precious gems, an intellectual
treasure which may fill in some of the gaps in our knowledge of a

people who lived thousands of years ago and which may have profound implications for the basis of some of our modern scientific knowledge. For some years now, it has been my opinion that there is so much that we could learn if we could understand the essential truth of the stories by peeling away the successive layers of embroidered embellishment and distortion with which constant retelling of the stories over the centuries has enveloped them. The intrinsic meaning of even the simplest of tales easily becomes distorted or lost altogether when the circumstances that forged the story no longer exist. In order to better illustrate this, perhaps it would be useful to quote an example from closer to home both in time and in distance.

There is a little verse like a nursery rhyme that is known to most children in England. Part of the verse goes:

'Oranges and lemons,' say the bells of St Clement's
'I owe you five farthings,' say the bells of St Martin's
'When will you pay me?' say the bells of Old Bailey
'When I grow rich,' say the bells of Shoreditch
'When will that be?' say the bells of Stepney
'I do not know,' say the great bells of Bow

But what is this all about? It is likely that not one person in a hundred would be able to say, despite the fact that the majority of them would know it word for word and could sing it all the way through – its accompanying tune is always learned with the words. The truth is, according to many experts, that this little verse and its attendant tune represent the sound of the peals of bells that could be heard from London's most famous churches. The verse dates to some time prior to the middle of the seventeenth century. Much of the City of London was destroyed in the Great Fire of 1666 and the churches in question were all rebuilt, the bells of which also had to be replaced and probably no longer sounded as they had before the fire. So here we have an important historical record which is carried around in the heads of most English people for their whole lives and most of them have no idea what it might mean. There are many other examples in English tradition and it is, of course, certain that they exist in other languages and cultures as well. The verse serves to illustrate the fact that it is very easy to learn a few lines of a 'song' without understanding its intrinsic meaning or even knowing that it has one.

In the case of this nursery rhyme, there was no intention on the part of its originator to deceive the listener in any way. On the contrary, the message is very clear – though nowadays only when the subject of the rhyme is explained. This is a salient point. Although many of the stories told round winter fires in classical Greece may have represented nothing more than the genius of a people who had learned to create what must be some of the most wonderful folk tales in the world, a few of the stories may have subtle undertones which, once understood, ring out as clearly to the listener as did the bells of those fine churches in London on many a crisp Sunday morning prior to the Great Fire of 1666.

In a way, I first came upon this possibility by accident. Nearly ten years ago, I had been called upon to offer a talk on the planet Jupiter and the supposed part it plays in astrology. Ever anxious to inform interested people on matters astronomical as well as the less scientifically acceptable astrology, I gathered together some facts and figures relating to the physical aspects of the planet. I started my search by looking in an encyclopaedia. Under the heading 'Jupiter', the writer told me what a remarkable coincidence it was that Jupiter had risen to the rank of father among the gods and goddesses, both for the Greeks who knew him as Zeus and later in a Latinised form for the Romans who called him Jupiter. The coincidence springs from the fact that the planet Jupiter is by far the largest planet in the solar system, so large in fact that its mass exceeds that of all the other planets put together.

This was indeed an odd coincidence. But then again, was this a coincidence or had the association between the planet, the name and the role of father to the other gods been made quite deliberately and for a good reason? Each of the planets known to the Greeks and Romans became associated with one of the gods or goddesses, and each one had held a particular significance. The puzzle was to work out a reasonable explanation for Jupiter's prominence in the pantheon. In the night sky, Jupiter is nothing like as bright as the evening and morning star, Venus. Jupiter's size, when viewed with the naked eye, is diminutive when compared with our own Moon because of its distance from Earth. And it is not really much brighter than the more remote of the super-giants,

Saturn. Jupiter is just not prominent in the night sky under even the best of atmospheric conditions.

At this point I started to look again at Greek mythology, only this time with slightly different eyes. What I discovered was such a graphic description of some of the more remote planets in our solar system that I was truly amazed that, to the best of my knowledge, these tales had never been looked at in this way before.

In fact, the story starts further out in space than with the position of the massive Jupiter: it actually starts with the planet Saturn. Saturn appears in Greek mythology a little earlier than Jupiter. My chief source of information is the Greek writer, Hesiod, to whom I am indebted. Hesiod was writing on the Greek mainland around the eighth century BC and is credited with being the father of didactic poetry. The *Theogony* is his account of the Creation according to Greek tradition. It is doubtful that Hesiod understood the implications of some of what he wrote in the *Theogony*, however, for he was merely endeavouring to compose an epic poem, encapsulating the most common stories known to the Greeks at the time. It is my opinion that he knew no more about the origin or accuracy of some of the observations than a twentieth-century child understands medieval London and its churches. How many of these tales came to mainland Greece from Minoan Crete is difficult to say with any certainty, although there are clues on Crete, especially relating to Saturn (the Greek Cronos) and Jupiter (the Greek Zeus) to show that many of them could have first been told in the cool recesses of the palaces of Knossos and Phaistos.

Hesiod's writing is flowery and in places quite tedious for he insists, like the Old Testament writers, on introducing us to every offshoot of the Greek pantheon of which there are thousands. The epic, for our purposes, starts with the introduction of Cronos. We are told that Cronos was the last of 12 children, who were known collectively as the Titans, born to Gaea (which translates as Earth) and Oranos (which literally means heaven). Cronos was the youngest of the Titans but arrived on the scene before Gaea and Oranos begat the remainder of their strange family. The second batch of infants were the Cyclops, three in number, each sporting only one eye in centre of their foreheads. Lastly came three more giants, each of whom had 50 heads and 100 arms.

Oranos was horrified by his hideous children and decided to

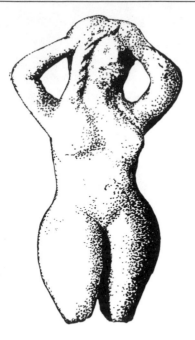

A representation of the earth goddess, Gaea.

hide them all in a secret place under the Earth. Perhaps understandably, this made Gaea not only uncomfortable but rather annoyed as well. In revenge, she created 'adamant' which is generally said to be iron. This she fashioned into what Hesiod variously describes as a 'sickle' or a 'scimitar' with which the Titans could overthrow their tyrannical father and escape from their prison under the Earth. Only Cronos had sufficient courage to undertake the enterprise and he lay in wait for Oranos. Cronos ambushed Oranos and castrated him with the sickle supplied by Gaea. Cronos is not too popular in the Greek traditions and Hesiod is not especially complimentary in his description of the god. The reason for this may be that Zeus, who was eventually to seize power from Cronos, was of supreme importance in Hesiod's time and therefore had to be seen to have had a good reason for overthrowing his father who was the more venerable of the two gods.

Following Cronos's overthrow of his father, Cronos freed the other Titans and with their aid became the ruler of all the gods. Unfortunately, he turned out to be as bad a tyrant as Oranos had been. Cronos was also very jealous of his position and on each occasion that his consort and sister, Rhea, gave birth to a child, he would promptly take the infant and swallow it. This fate befell five children, by which time Rhea appears to have decided that enough was enough. After the birth of her sixth child, Zeus, she presented Cronos with a large stone in place of the infant and entrusted the care of Zeus to a she-goat, safe on the Earth in the Dikte Mountains of Crete. Cronos duly swallowed the stone without inspecting it, leaving Zeus to grow up unmolested and ultimately to overthrow Cronos in a great fight which we are told shook the very vaults of heaven itself.

One consequence of Zeus's rise to power was that he was able to force Cronos into regurgitating the children his father had swallowed. Henceforth, they became the staunchest supporters of their younger brother and were ultimately listed among the most important and oldest members of the Greek pantheon. Hesiod relates that, when the time came for Zeus to unseat his father, the young god cast about the family of gods already in existence for supporters. The goddess Styx offered her own four children as supporters to the new order. They are named as the gods Power and Force and the goddesses Victory and Glory. In his description of Zeus's reaction to this service Hesiod is quite specific, for he relates that henceforth these four 'have no house apart from Zeus, nor any path except where God commands them and they sit forever at the side of thundering Zeus'.

On Crete, not far from the Dikte cave associated with the birth of Zeus, there is another cave which is named for his father Cronos. Also worthy of note are the Cyclops, brothers of Cronos, hidden along with the Titans and the 50-headed giants in the Earth. There are strong folk traditions in Crete related to the Cyclops which are supposed at one time to have inhabited the southern coast of the island, there to waylay and eat all passers-by who were not wary of their presence. When gazing on the marvellous fortifications of the Mycenaean empire, later Greek chroniclers came to know them as the Cyclopedian walls. The general explanation for this name these days is that the writers in question, seeing these vast ramparts with their huge stones for the first time, considered that only giants, such as the Cyclops, could have possessed sufficient strength to erect them. It should be remembered, however, that these fortifications were almost certainly built under the supervision of Minoan engineers who served the Mycenaeans after the fall of

Minoan Crete around 1450 BC. It seems likely that the Minoan association with the Cyclops may have been the reason that the walls were so named.

Apart from the Dikte connection, there is another link between Zeus and Crete: the young god was suckled by a she-goat. The goat was sacred to the Minoans and may have been of greater importance before the rise of the bull worship on the island. Despite Crete's fall from prominence after about 1450 BC, no Greek writer seems to have strayed from the idea that Zeus originally came from Crete. The tales relating to Cronos and Zeus are almost certainly two of the oldest stories in Greek mythology because the mighty Zeus is already the undisputed king of heaven in all the other tales. Only in the part of the creation myth associated with the rise of Cronos do we find traditions that may be older.

If there are enough connections between Zeus and Crete to attribute these stories to a Cretan origin, then any astronomical significance that they have must surely be a strong indication that they are also Cretan and, therefore, Minoan. I was immediately struck by a curious parallel with the behaviour of the planets of our solar system and the behaviour of the gods in Hesiod's tales. There was an apparent symbolism in Hesiod's stories that strongly suggested that the tales were actually describing planetary movements. The first clues that led me to this possibility were the way in which Hesiod kept referring to Cronos as 'crooked' and the nature of the weapon with which he castrated Oranos – a sickle. Both could point to the original storytellers' recognition of the existence of Cronos's (Saturn's) ring system. The weapon used by Cronos is never referred to as a 'sword' or a 'dagger'; Hesiod makes it quite clear that the weapon had a curved blade and seems to avoided any ambiguity that might have arisen if he had referred to the weapon as a sword – some Greek swords were curved but others were straight.

An observer of Saturn using a moderately-sized telescope could be forgiven for failing to understand the nature of the planet's ring system. It is, in fact, composed of innumerable particles of different sizes spread out in a wide plane round the planet's equator, extending thousands of miles out into space. Although very wide, the rings have little depth, which is why we only have a good view of them when the planet's orientation relative to the Earth is such that they show their apparently flat surface to us. When the rings are side-on to the Earth, they are very difficult, if not impossible, to see. Thus only after watching the planet for some time while the planet's orientation changed would the thinness of the ring system become obvious to an observer. As the rings became more side-on to the Earth, the visible part illuminated by the Sun would appear very like a crescent. Moreover, it is never possible to see that part of the rings that extends round the back of the planet and so they always tend to have a sickle-like appearance. The analogy of a curved blade is easy to understand.

Saturn has a great many moons. Until the advent of powerful modern telescopes, however, it was thought to have only five. This is precisely the number of children swallowed by Cronos. It is my belief that in the swallowing and regurgitating of Cronos's children we have the perfect description of the behaviour of a planet's moons which disappear from view and reappear some time later. We know now, of course, that we can see a moon when it passes across the face of a planet or when its orbit extends beyond the planet's face. We are also aware that it will pass out of sight for a while as it goes behind the planet's disc, eventually to emerge again on the other side. Less enlightened souls could be forgiven for believing that the moon was being 'eaten' by the planet, for only with a true knowledge of the workings of planetary orbits does the truth of the moon's temporary disappearance become obvious.

We find a similar situation in the case of Zeus, where the explanation of the behaviour of the moons is even more lucid. The four children of Styx could easily be meant to represent Jupiter's four largest moons which are known as the Galilean moons, so-called because it was the Italian astronomer and supposed inventor of the telescope, Galileo, who first observed the moons with the aid of a telescope. Hesiod clearly wanted it to be known that the four children of Styx always attend Zeus. And indeed they must, if we are to see them as the Galilean moons, for it is certain that wherever the planet goes, the moons will always follow and that whatever house (in the zodiac) he occupies, they will also be in that same place.

As far as planetary knowledge is concerned, it was clear to me that Hesiod's descriptions were only the tip of the iceberg, though the Greek folk-tales he included in the *Theogony* are the only ones that can be said to have a Cretan origin. But we must not forget that the Minoans were great travellers and it would be surprising if they had failed to pass their astronomical knowledge on to other peoples they encountered. Is it possible that the mythologies of other peoples in the Mediterranean show that they too had a conception of the size and importance of Jupiter and Saturn?

Immediately prior to the invention of a reliable chronometer in the eighteenth century, accurate navigation at sea had proved to be a thorn in the side of would-be explorers. Oceanic exploration depends upon a good knowledge of one's true position, as we have already seen, and it is essential to have an accurate timekeeping device that can be checked against local time in order to establish one's position east or west of a given point. There had been an alternative method for ascertaining 'absolute time', however, and it only fell into disuse after the invention of the chronometer. This method relied upon an observation of the major moons of Jupiter, those same children of the goddess Styx. It was originally devised by Galileo in the seventeenth century – or was it?

Under good conditions, these four moons are just about visible to the naked eye, though for all useful purposes a telescope of some sort would be necessary to track them with any degree of precision. They have an interesting relationship with each other and differ in their orbital periods. The moon Io is closest to Jupiter, having an orbital period of only 1.77 days, while Callisto, furthest of the four from Jupiter, takes 16.69 days to complete one journey round its host. By observing when these four moons are periodically eclipsed by the body of Jupiter itself, it is possible to gain a fairly good reckoning of 'absolute time' which would remain the same on any part of the Earth. The reason that this is possible is because of Jupiter's distance from the Earth. Moreover, unlike our own Moon, Jupiter's moons are in no way affected by the Earth.

The possibility of using the Phaistos Disc to plot the changes in the position of Jupiter's moons has not been explored. More analysis is required before this could be undertaken. However, if eighteenth-century sailors could track and use the moons of Jupiter to gain a knowledge of absolute time, then, assuming they had a telescope, so could the Minoans. If the Minoans had telescopes, they would have been able to establish absolute time and they would have had all the requirements to establish both longitude and latitude at any point on the surface of the Earth. A Minoan form of telescope would also help to explain how it was possible for them to have acquired so much knowledge about the solar system.

The problem, of course, is that the Minoans did not possess a telescope and they would not have been able to discern all that much about Saturn, Jupiter or their moons with the naked eye alone. It is generally accepted that the optical telescope was not invented until the seventeenth century and that the inventor was Galileo.

CHAPTER SIXTEEN

ASTRONOMY AND MYTHOLOGY

There is a definite relationship between many of the mythologies and early religions of Western Europe; these probably date from around the late Stone Age or the early Bronze Age. These are meticulously dealt with by Robert Graves in *The White Goddess*. Graves finds evidence for an evolving, mystical alphabet which is mainly based on various aspects of tree-worship. Graves is also able to demonstrate many of the cultural associations that existed across Europe during the Bronze Age and he often mentions the embryonic state of Greece and the Minoan civilisation of Crete.

There are many examples of art from Minoan Crete which would tend to indicate that a form of nature-worship particularly associated with trees was practised on the island during the Bronze Age. Archaeological finds indicate that the same sort of practices took place far to the west in Ireland and in innumerable cultures in between. Similar indications can be found in Nordic mythology although the lands of the Norsemen were separated from ancient Crete by thousands of miles and by many centuries. In fact, the observance of the Nordic beliefs extended well into the Christian era, the inevitability of the ever-spreading new religion of Christianity only gradually being accepted by many kings and warlords. There are many gravestones, some of them as late as the eleventh century AD, that carry Christian symbolism on one side and scenes from Nordic mythology on the other. The influence of Odin and Thor was not completely eradicated, however, as they are still remembered in the names of the days of the week: Wednesday – Odin's day, Thursday – Thor's day, Friday – Frigg's day; (Frigg was Odin's wife).

147

For countless years the tales of epic deeds and warrior gods were transmitted orally. It was only comparatively recently that any of the Norse sagas were written down. Many of them relate the real events of peoples who ranged far and wide in their longships. One of the best recorders of these epics was a man by the name of Snorri Sturluson, an Icelander who lived between 1179 and 1241. In his work the *Prose Edda*, Sturluson gives a comprehensive account of the creation according to the Norse traditions. In the Norse tradition, the responsibilities of Zeus (the sky god is known in almost all mythologies in one form or another) were split between Odin and Thor, though it is also evident that with the passage of time Thor acquired some of the characteristics formerly associated with the planet Mars. Thor, like Zeus, was the thunderer. He had four sons, Modi, Magni, Prudr and Ullr. The first three of these can be fairly reliably translated to mean Fierce Courage, Colossal Might, and Strength, none of which are a million miles away from the Power, Force, Victory and Glory of Greek mythology, although Victory and Glory were, of course, goddesses.

At one stage in the sagas, Thor fights a terrible battle during which a whetstone is hurled at him, a piece of which hits him on the head. Is it stretching credibility too far to suggest that this might be related in some way to the Great Red Spot of Jupiter? The Great Red Spot is a huge anticyclonic storm that is readily viewed with a moderately powerful telescope. Although the intensity of the colour of the spot changes from time to time, it is at least 300 years old and may have been even more evident in ancient times.

Wearing his Martian coat as the God of War, Thor is said to have sported a huge red beard and to have had a chariot pulled by two goats which he could eat but which would magically reappear to pull his chariot once more. Mars is well known as the Red Planet because of its colour. It has two moons. As in the Greek myths, these could be said to be eaten by the planet, later to be brought back to life again when they appear from the far side of the planet's disc. In some of the sagas, Odin, who is synonymous with Saturn and Cronos, is described as being an old man 'with a broad-brimmed hat'. Once again, this may be an allusion to the rings of Saturn for which a broad-brimmed hat is a good metaphor.

These examples from Nordic mythology show how the myth patterns of pre-Christian peoples carried symbolism associated with the superior planets of the solar system similar to that which may have already been old when Hesiod wrote down the tales in the *Theogony*. If Hesiod had little idea of the real content of some of these stories, it is highly unlikely that the compilers of the sagas had any better notion.

Apart from the ancient Greeks and the later Norsemen, other cultures that were more or less contemporary with the Minoans seem to have had mythologies that were similarly associated with the heavens in a way that suggests that they were based on observation of the behaviour of the planets and their moons. To the Babylonians, for example, the great sky god was known as Marduk, an early counterpart of Zeus. His war chariot was pulled by 'four fiery steeds' which could be a reference to the four major moons of the super-giant Jupiter. In fact, the association of the number four with the sky god is almost universal. It is also to be found as far away as the New World where Central American cultures had similar beliefs. In our own culture, which relies heavily on Hebrew mythology from the Old Testament of the Bible, we find the throne of God surrounded by the four archangels, Gabriel, Uriel, Michael and Raphael. The struggle between Cronos and Zeus is also preserved in these accounts; Satan (whose name is very close to that of Saturn, even if experts disagree about the origin of the word) is cast down into hell by Jehovah who in this instance at least seems to owe much to the old sky god of early belief.

Some of the most compelling evidence comes from the continent of Africa and a little known tribe called the Dogon. They occupy a region of what is now Sudan and were extensively studied back in the late 1940s by two French anthropologists, Griaule and Dieterlan. They discovered that the Dogon were aware of the behaviour of the planets Jupiter and Saturn and probably had been aware of their behaviour for hundreds and possibly for thousands of years. They were able to describe the planets in great detail. These mysterious people represented Saturn as a dot surrounded by a circle. Jupiter, on the other hand, was a dot surrounded by four smaller dots. There was a pun associated with the Dogon name for Jupiter and the name of a plant which they knew as the *sene*. The reason for the association, the tribe elders were only too willing to point out, was that the sene plant has a twisted stem which they associated with the movement of the moons of Jupiter. It appears that they understood the rather complex motion of a planet's satellite which, in addition to orbiting its host, is also moving round the sun in the orbit of the planet so that its movement in space is actually a spiral.

It has often been suggested that the Dogon possessed information that had been explained to them by earlier missionaries to the area, who would almost certainly have understood such matters. However, there is one fact here that does not bear out this supposition. Like the Egyptians of old, who may well have been the original source of the Dogon information, the tribe were almost obsessed with the importance of the star Sirius. Its significance to the Egyptians in connection with the flooding of the Nile is well known. Sirius has a central part to play in Dogon mythology and religion. The Dogon had always represented Sirius as a large dot with a much smaller dot by the side of it. The anthropologists were informed by the Dogon that the reason for this was that Sirius had a companion. As far as modern astronomers are concerned, Sirius B was not discovered until 1862 although its existence had been predicted in 1844. Griaule and Dieterlan remained convinced that the Dogon belief in Sirius B must have predated its modern discovery, so deeply was its existence etched into their rituals.

How this supposedly primitive people, or any other culture prior to the advent of optical or radio astronomy, could have been aware of the existence of Sirius B will probably remain a mystery for ever. It may be possible that for reasons we do not presently understand, the second star was at one time visible with the naked eye, though this has certainly not been the case in recent centuries. What this information does imply, however, is that the religious patterns of the Dogon, encapsulating a knowledge of the rings of Saturn and the moons of Jupiter, may well be far older than the arrival of the first Christian missionaries to Africa.

The above examples are not the only cultures to have had a knowledge of the four moons of Jupiter and encapsulated it in their mythology. There are many others. Nowhere is it more pronounced, however, than in the stories that originated in ancient Greece, nor is it restricted to those tales written down for the first time by Hesiod. For ancient knowledge of the physical dimensions of Jupiter, we need look no further than the *Iliad*, probably the

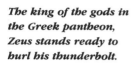

The king of the gods in the Greek pantheon, Zeus stands ready to hurl his thunderbolt.

most famous of the works of Homer. In the *Iliad,* Zeus says: 'I am mightiest of all. Make trial that you may know. Fasten a rope of gold to heaven and lay hold, every god and goddess. You could not drag down Zeus. But if I wished to drag you down, then I would. The rope I would bind to a pinnacle of Olympus and all would hang in air, yes, the very earth and the sea too.' Does this statement indicate that the Greeks knew that Jupiter was greater in mass than all the other planets put together? It certainly appears to substantiate this theory. If they were aware of Jupiter's mass, they must have had a good understanding of the solar system and of mathematics to be able to assess the mass of heavenly bodies so far from the Earth.

There is other information from Greece and its surrounding regions that would seem to attest to a far better understanding of astronomy than we have previously assumed of the peoples of the Aegean and eastern Mediterranean in ancient times. Democritus, born around 470 BC, was a Greek philosopher of the Eleatic school. He stated that the Milky Way (our galaxy), formerly said to have been drops of milk from the bosom of Juno, was in fact composed of innumerable stars that were too small to be distinguished by the naked eye. If this was an educated guess, we can only bow our knee to the great Democritus who can surely have had no way of knowing the truth of his assertion unless, of course, he had observed the fact for himself. (Of course, it only appears that the stars are too small; they are difficult to distinguish with the naked eye because they are so far away from us and it is the vast distances involved that makes them appear so tiny.)

Another revelation comes from closer to home. In Jonathan Swift's account of Gulliver's visit to Laputa, the flying island in *Gulliver's Travels*, he wrote a very accurate description of the moons of Mars, including a good estimation of their orbital characteristics. The odd thing about this is that Swift wrote *Gulliver's Travels* in 1726 but the moons of Mars were not discovered until the American astronomer Professor Hall observed them 150 years later in 1877. Either Swift was uncannily prescient or he gained his knowledge about the moons of Mars from a source that is now unknown to us. Jonathan Swift was something of an expert in classical studies so it is very likely that he found the information relating to Mars and its moons during his studies of ancient writings.

Classical Greece seems to have been the focal point for many of these astronomically-based legends. However, there is little evidence to suggest that the ancient Greeks had a complete understanding of the astronomical knowledge that was seemingly available to them. The astronomical information that is evident in the stories is only revealed in snippets, implying that these learned men merely nibbled at the edges of astronomy without really coming to terms with the full implications of the stories. It seems likely that many of the stories were handed on from culture to culture and that many of them may well have started life in the mountains and plains of ancient Crete.

What is more, there is evidence, not only from Crete but from other places as well, to suggest that the telescope may not have been an invention of Renaissance Europe after all. This evidence suggests that it was, in fact, a very much older invention.

CHAPTER SEVENTEEN

THE TELESCOPE – AN ANCIENT INVENTION?

S o far, no archaeologist has unearthed the remains of a telescope from ancient times. The reasons are fairly obvious. Even if such devices did exist thousands of years ago, the complicated requirements of their manufacture would make them quite rare; very few would have been made and this in itself lessens the chance of one surviving. For much the same reason, broken pottery is much more likely to be found on an archaeological site than jewellery made from precious metals and gems – pottery was much more common than jewellery. In addition, the body of any such device would almost certainly have been constructed of wood which decays very readily. Another reason why such a discovery has not been made could be attributable to the fact that archaeology has only recently become the painstaking and careful science that it is today. Moreover, since the only parts of an ancient telescope that would be likely to survive the ravages of time would be the lenses and perhaps a few metal fittings, the find could easily be misidentified as something else. And it is a sad truth that one does not find what one considers to be an impossibility; and an ancient telescope would be an impossibility for many archaeologists.

The rings of Saturn, its five major moons, the moons of Jupiter and an appreciation of the planet's true dimensions, as well as the two small moons of Mars are all indiscernible to naked-eye observation although, arguably, the moons of Jupiter are just visible to the naked eye under very special conditions. If we are to suggest that the wealth of information encapsulated in the early Greek myths does in fact show that the Greeks, or an earlier culture from whom they learned the stories, appreciated the astronomical truths discussed in the last chapter, then it is reasonable to suggest that telescopes did exist in the distant past. It is always difficult to throw off prejudices that have been built into us during our education. Like Archimedes jumping out of his bath with the famous cry of *'Eureka!'*, or Stevenson watching a kettle boil and instantly inventing the steam engine, Galileo's invention of the telescope in 1609 is something we have all been taught. In fact, Galileo did not invent the refracting telescope at all but improved upon what already existed and had existed for some time. Indeed the telescope was not invented by an Italian scientist but probably by a Dutch navigator.

It should not be assumed that the materials for building a telescope did not exist 4,000 years ago; indeed, the means can be viewed in many museums throughout the world. The Cairo Museum in Egypt has lenses, both of glass and of rock crystal, which date back thousands of years. Another exists in the British Museum. This one is made of rock crystal, is accurately ground and comes from Helwan in Egypt. The English scientist Sir David Brewster (1781–1848) displayed, at an exhibition in Bedford, a lens which came from Nineveh in Mesopotamia. Nineveh flourished in the centuries prior to 600 BC.

Rock crystal lenses are easily distinguishable from glass lenses because they do not deteriorate significantly during the time that they spend in the ground whereas glass ones do. The basements and storage areas of many museums could contain a wealth of ancient glass lenses, many of which are so damaged or have deteriorated so much that their true purpose is now beyond easy recognition. Glass is not a recent innovation by any means. The Greek comic poet Aristophanes informs us that 'glass spheres' could be purchased in Athens around 460 BC. Glass windows, almost as good as modern ones, have been unearthed in the Roman town of Pompeii which was destroyed in AD 63. What is more, innovations may have surpassed common glass, for it is known that the Roman Emperor Tiberius, who reigned around the time of Christ, ordered an inventor to be put to death because he had managed to perfect the art of making 'pliable glass', on the dubious pretext that the Emperor considered such a revolutionary idea should go no further.

It is known that Ptolomy III, who was born in 281 BC, had a device mounted on a lighthouse in Alexandria with which ships at a great distance could be observed. In the New World, rock crystal was worked to stunning effect. Although no lenses have been found in the Americas, a wonderful rock crystal skull fashioned from one piece of crystal and weighing 5.2 kg (11.5 lb) was found in Lubaanton in Belize. There are no marks on the object to betray how it was made; it represents a masterpiece of early art. Any craftsman capable of making this superb skull with its many complex contours would have had little difficulty creating a usable lens.

What Central and South America might lack in hard evidence, is made up for linguistically. *The Lexicon* is a book written by a Dominican monk, one Domingo de San Thomas. It was published in 1560 and is a sort of Quiche Indian and Spanish dictionary. On page 132 of the book we find the word *'quilpi'* which from the Spanish translation literally means 'an optical instrument for looking into the distance'. The word *quilpi* is also associated with the Quiche words for 'planet' and 'cosmic system'. It is likely that if the Quiche Indians had managed to manufacture such a device – and if the word was in common usage they almost certainly had – the Spaniards would have most likely destroyed it. The Spanish conquistadors destroyed many things from the American cultures that they overthrew, especially if they believed that the objects were sacrilegious in the eyes of the Catholic Church. Anything to do with the heavens would have fallen into this category. Galileo discovered to his own cost, some decades later, that the Catholic Church did not take kindly to any suggestion that the solar system did not conform to the dogmas of the Church.

The Minoans were quite capable of making lenses; there is one on display in Heraklion Museum and it is known to be of Minoan manufacture. It is assumed that it was used by craftsmen making the delicate seals of which so many have been found on Crete, a lot of which are very small and would have required astounding eyesight on the part of the maker if no optical aid had been available. It seems quite within the bounds of possibility that a craftsman capable of turning out lenses on a regular basis might have put two of them together to find out whether he could improve on the magnification he achieved with only one. Once this experiment had been tried, it would have been but a simple step to use the two lenses to look at objects others than seals.

There have been too many writers this century who, faced with the anomalies thrown up by chance discoveries and fantastic writings from the past, have been quick to assert that early man was in some way helped by extraterrestrials with superior intelligence. This is highly insulting to the intellectual and creative abilities of our ancient ancestors. Moreover, such speculative explanations are hardly necessary, particularly in the case of early astronomy, since even the most learned of ancient societies appear to have known no more about the solar system than we ourselves did until about a century or two ago. Although it is speculated that some early cultures were aware of the existence of the planet Uranus, which is just about visible with the naked eye, it would seem that Saturn with its moons and rings was as far as their technology could reach. This demolishes the 'alien influence' theory, since travellers from distant stars must surely have a comprehensive knowledge of our entire solar system rather than one that only stretched as far as Saturn. Moreover, it is wrong to assume that people living in Crete 4,000 years ago were any less intelligent than we are today.

Gunter D. Rothes, in his work *Handbook of Planet Observers,* is of the opinion that, in order to resolve the rings and moons of Saturn, an optical telescope with lenses of about 13 centimetres (5 inches) in diameter is desirable. Other experts reckon on something smaller, perhaps just under 10 centimetres (4 inches). By modern standards, this is a fairly modest size of telescope, though to people of 4,000 years ago with limited technology this may have been beyond their abilities to construct. However, under the right atmospheric conditions and in the best locations, a much smaller apparatus might have achieved the same results as, say, a 10 centimetre telescope. It would not have been easy and continued observation may have been difficult but that does not mean that it was impossible.

The possibility of the astronomers of Minoan Crete having had access to primitive telescopes is a radical departure from orthodox beliefs, though it would answer many of the questions that have arisen as a result of the interpretation of the Phaistos Disc that I am proposing here. The fact that the existence of such devices has not been confirmed by the discovery of what are clearly the remains of early telescopes that date from Minoan times should not be interpreted as meaning that such devices did not exist. Apart from anything else, one cannot prove a negative. If knowledge about the behaviour of the planets and their moons had existed in Minoan Crete, it would have been in the hands of the élite so that when the Minoan civilisation ended in about 1450 BC much of the knowledge they had accumulated may well have died with them. The knowledge that did outlive the Minoans perhaps only survived in a fragmentary form. And that knowledge may or may not have included how to make a telescope.

As far as the legends relating to Cronos and Zeus are concerned, we have no way of knowing if these represented the imaginative attempts of a people trying to make sense out of something they could see but did not understand, or whether they were a means of passing on astronomical information from one generation to another. It is entirely possible that these stories were the working principles of a closely guarded sect whose members passed on the truth about astronomical observations and mathematics in a way that only they understood. At some point, the chain was broken and the stories became the myths and legends that we know today.

We can never know just how old the myths associated with the sky god and the older god who represents his father in the Greek myths really are. It is not even beyond the realms of possibility that this information springs from a yet older source and that parts of it may have been as much of a mystery to the Minoans as it turned out to be to successive cultures. If we assume that the Greek myths are indeed imaginative descriptions of the behaviour of the planets and moons in our solar system, many of them would have to be renamed accordingly. Although Jupiter's and Saturn's moons have the names of Greek gods and heroes, most of these were bestowed on them during the seventeenth and eighteenth centuries and are not the ones ascribed to them by the ancient Greeks.

CHAPTER EIGHTEEN

WORSHIP AND RITUAL

It is clear that the nature goddess who was responsible for the fertility and growth of the crops was the principal deity in Minoan Crete. In early Cretan art, there are numerous examples of what appears to be the goddess, usually portrayed with large breasts and often with a protruding stomach, symbolising pregnancy and therefore fertility. The first examples of such religious figures are extremely crude, showing no more skill in their creation than can be observed in similar ancient examples found elsewhere in Western Europe. Gradually, however, as the light of Minoan culture spread its creative brilliance across the fertile plains of Crete, these representations of the Mother Goddess became ever more beautiful. A late example of this evolution can be seen on page 160. What spurred on this artistic growth is not known.

Another and probably even more important source of information concerning the beliefs of the Minoans can be found on the many hundreds of so-called seals that archaeological excavations have brought to light. Often these depict natural scenes with animals such as wild goats, lions and birds. Sometimes, however, they show a brief glimpse of an aspect of Minoan life or mythology. Many of the scenes are difficult to interpret, especially those that show offerings being made to a figure who is usually a woman and often seated under a tree. Does this figure represent the goddess, or a priestess or queen who is taking on the role of the goddess for a particular festival? Fortunately there are some scenes which can be interpreted without too much difficulty. These show a figure flanked by mythical creatures and there is little doubt that the figure is meant to be the goddess.

A snake goddess discovered at the palace of Knossos.

It seems likely that Minoan beliefs centred upon a duality: a goddess and a god representing the female and the male. The god took on different forms in his appearances on the seals and these may have been related to the ritual year. At first he is a child but later he becomes the consort of the goddess. The birth of the god, his subsequent association with the goddess figure and his ultimate demise are all undoubtedly connected with the cycle of nature which is an aspect of religion seen in many cultures. The female represents the perpetual aspect of nature, whereas the young god who becomes her consort and then dies is symbolic of the ephemeral quality of life – birth, death and rebirth.

The tree is often included in these scenes and is undoubtedly connected with nature and seasonal rebirth. The tree in Minoan art is also reminiscent of the World Tree that figures in so many ancient religions: the roots reach down to the underworld and the branches extend into heaven. In some beliefs, the many boughs of this tree contain the realms of men and the realms of gods and we may see in the Minoan tree-worship a form of belief that eventually became important to the peoples of Northern Europe for many centuries before their conversion to Christianity. In Crete, tree-worship probably focused on the olive tree, a species that tends to live for a very long time. Two thousand years of fruitful life is not impossible. To the Minoans, the long-lived olive could have represented immortality.

The Minoans often appear to have encapsulated many of mankind's most ancient beliefs. This is true of their reverence for bulls. Bull-worship may have achieved its zenith in Minoan Crete. In Minoan times, the bull was wild, ferocious and dangerous. This animal played an important part in Minoan rituals. Its horns are to be seen everywhere in Minoan art and architecture, although they changed over time from naturalistic images into stylised representations. The first civilisations sprang up in the fertile plains between the Tigres and the Euphrates and these seem to have revered the bull. Throughout history, cultures have displayed a propensity for bovine worship. There are instances in the Old Testament which show that even the leaders of the first Jewish kingdom had some difficulty preventing a resurgence of bull-worship. Mithraism, an ancient religion based on a worship of Mithras the 'son of the living Sun', that was eventually swept away by Christianity in the fourth century AD, equated the sacrificial sacred white bull with Mithras. Mithras retained the connection between the celestial quality of the sky god, the Sun and the sacred bull. This reverence for the bull has survived right up to our own time. Hindus still retain a special reverence for cattle, which wander unmolested through the streets of Indian towns and cities. To eat beef is unthinkable to Hindus.

Another example of early bull worship comes from the Hittite empire (c. 1650–1200 BC). A god, possibly a sky god of the later Zeus type, is depicted riding a wild bull, carrying forked lightning in one hand and a double-headed axe in the other. This was a form of symbolism that would have been clearly understood by the Minoans, for the sky god was undoubtedly an essential part of their religious beliefs. Variations of this theme can be seen all over Europe from the Bronze Age onwards. Zeus was the most common

161

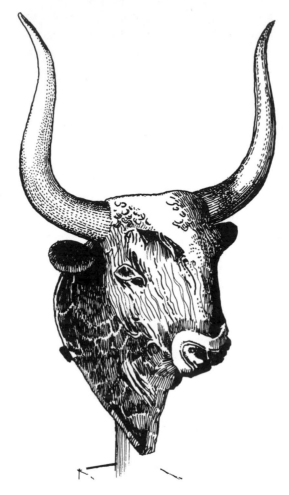

A sacred bull's head displays the animal's magnificent horns, weapons it would use against the athletes in the bull games.

name for the god above all gods but he was also known as Ahura Mazda, Marduk, Jupiter, Thor and possibly by a hundred other names by the peoples of Europe and Asia. His worship only ceased with the rise of Christianity, though vestiges have survived and can be seen in modern Jewish and Christian beliefs. If the bull was the chosen means of transportation for the sky god, he may well have been equated with the Sun. Statues of bulls and cows from Egypt often depict the animals carrying the solar disc between their wide horns.

There is some uncertainty concerning the association between all these disparate components of ancient religions, though elements of them can be found in the antecedents of nearly all world beliefs and bull-worship may be one of the oldest. Large wild bulls are included among some of the finest Stone Age cave paintings. Perhaps the power and virility of these creatures played some part in their being etched into the psyche of mankind far back in the mists of time.

Minoan Crete is famous for its bull games. These involved young athletes, males and females alike, performing dangerous gymnastics around the bodies and heads of ferocious wild bulls. This is almost certainly the origin of the legend of the Minotaur, the half-man, half-bull who was supposed to live within the labyrinth. It is even possible that the groups of young men and women supposed to have been sent to Crete from the mainland ostensibly to be sacrificed to the Minotaur were, in reality, destined for training in the dangerous business of the bull games. It is not known how frequently the bull games were held but the solar associations of the bull with the midwinter solstice would suggest that this was when they were held. They may also have been held at midsummer and at the time of the spring and autumn equinoxes. Many people may have lost their lives during these performances and it is possible that the bulls were sacrificed after the entertainment. Bull games have survived into the present day in the form of bull-fighting and the famous Pamplona festival in which young bulls run freely through the streets, chasing the young men who test their skill and agility in avoiding these dangerous creatures. Perhaps the bull athletes of Crete were not forced into their profession at all.

The struggle to outwit an enraged bull may have been representative of man's efforts to tame the forces of nature. It could also have been perceived as a way of absorbing the bull's life-force into the individuals who participated in the games, a form of contagious magic (so-called because the magical influence operates by the person coming into physical contact with the magical object, no matter how brief the contact). This is a complex subject. In Greek mythology, we find Zeus becoming a white bull for an amorous liaison that resulted in the half-man, half-bull Minotaur. Of course, an all-powerful sky god could take on any form he desired, though there may be vestiges of even older beliefs encapsulated within this story and it is a tale shot through with Bronze Age metaphor.

The sacred horns could have developed into something much

more than a simple religious symbol, particularly since they were obviously associated with the solar disc. The Minoans reproduced them in stone and plaster along the roof lines of their palaces, particularly at Knossos. The Minoan astronomer priests had a good understanding of the timing of the solar year and could regulate their calendar more accurately than we choose to regulate our own. The knowledge necessary to do this could only have come about as a result of long observation and the palaces would have been a good place from which to make the observations. The excavations conducted by Sir Arthur Evans indicated that sacred horns adorned parts of the roof lines, and provided they were located at appropriate places (for example, if they fringed the eastern and western flanks of the palace) they may have been used for solar observations.

The orientation of the palace at Knossos would fit this idea quite nicely; it is arranged slightly east of north to slightly west of south. This might indicate a midwinter alignment. With a sufficiently uncluttered and distant horizon, the Sun would have been seen to rise within the frame formed by the sacred horns at some stage during the year, if observed from a fixed point on the far side of the flat roof. Much would have depended on the size of the solar disc at dawn and, of course, the dimensions of the sacred horns would have had to have been suitable if the Sun's body was to fit neatly between them. However, it would have been relatively simple to have arranged a row of sacred horns for monitoring the Sun's north–south passage throughout the year, with midsummer, midwinter and equinox positions all showing the solar disc at dawn neatly between the horns. Distant hills or mountains may also have been used as sighting points for more accurate observations. The mound on which Knossos stands has been shown to have been inhabited for centuries prior to Minoan times and may already have been a solar sighting point. Accurate times for the rise of planets, constellations and important fixed stars could also have been obtained in this way, especially if the zodiac was already known.

Undoubtedly all of this would have played an important part in the beliefs of the inhabitants of Crete. There would have been no distinction between religion, mathematics and astronomy for Bronze Age peoples. They would have been one and the same thing. There would have been many reasons why it would have

*Outside the palace at Knossos, a modern bull's-
born image illustrates bow the Minoans may
bave used the borns as sighting posts for solar
positions at specific times.*

been useful to the Minoans to understand the intricacies of solar,
lunar and zodiac interaction especially if it was believed that the
phenomena they observed were caused by a god. For example,
many early societies strove to understand and accurately predict
the timing of solar and lunar eclipses. These were of supreme
importance and it was believed that when they occurred it was a
time of great foreboding. The right rituals had to be performed in
order to avoid the almost certain disaster that was thought to
follow if the rituals were not observed.

The form of the necessary rituals that were observed by the
Minoans can only be surmised from surviving seals and frescos on
the palace walls. Most seem to have been supervised by women
who were probably priestesses. There are examples of frescos and
pottery showing dances, suggesting that the Minoans loved to
dance. It is quite probable that the dances formed part of the
rituals. There must also have been a good deal of blood-letting in
the form of animal sacrifices but there is no evidence to suggest the
barbarity that attended some earlier and many later pagan beliefs.

There were doubtless celebrations surrounding the quarters of
the year in Crete as elsewhere in Europe. It is known that fires were

165

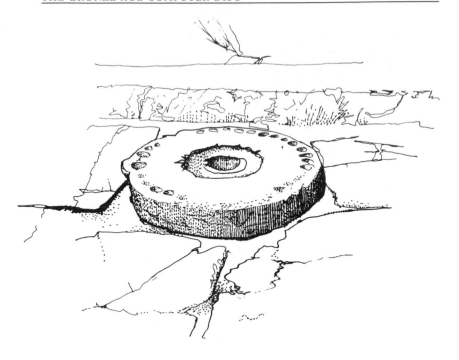

A votive stone: offerings of oil would be poured into the indentations around the circumference.

lit periodically on mountain tops and archaeologists have also discovered that votive offerings were thrown into the flames. There may have been a therapeutic element in the form of sympathetic magic to such celebrations, for models of parts of human limbs were included in the offerings – a prayer to the god for healing, perhaps.

The mountains were especially important to the Minoans in their religious beliefs. This is not surprising when one considers the isolation and tranquillity of the Cretan mountains. These same stark crags are the scenes of violent summer storms where lightning strikes hurl trees to the ground and the rumble of the sky god's thunder rolls round the echoing heights for hours. It was to caves within these mountains that the Minoans went. Some of the grottoes were dedicated to the various aspects of the goddess. These 'wombs of the Earth' with their impressive stalactites and stalagmites attracted thousands of votive offerings, among which

166

were sacred horns, statues, bronze and gold double axes and food. It was in such a cave as this in the Dikte Mountains that the great sky god Zeus was supposed to have been born and kept safe from his father, Cronos, who sought to devour him as he had all his other children. Other caves were sacred to the childbirth aspects of the goddess.

Many historians see no logical order in the pantheon of Minoan gods, unlike the gods of later classical Greece, although some of these were of Minoan origin; in Homer and Hesiod there are references to gods and goddesses who were certainly Minoan. The Minoans may have seen all deities as essentially manifestations of only one male and one female divinity, while in classical Greece the gods and goddesses acquired greater independence of existence, becoming more specialised in their areas of influence. They were given a wealth of different names. In this way, an early form of monotheism gradually turned into polytheism with a large family of gods and goddesses who were seen as entities in their own right, with the old sky god at the head.

Although the Minoans enjoyed bright colours, ornamentation and dance, they were a sensible and hard-working people; they also knew how to get things done. During the centuries that Knossos, Phaistos and Malia flourished, there was time enough for play and doubtless for prayer too. These were intelligent people, anxious to know how the world worked and keen to translate its secrets into a better life. Look at the huge human eyes that were painted on to pots and frescos by Minoan artists. Those eyes were used to gaze at the world and its marvels but they were also turned towards the wide and starry skies of Crete – and what they saw was used to forge a legacy for the world. Until now, there has been nobody to relate the story – that was before at least some of the secrets of the Phaistos Disc were revealed.

CHAPTER NINETEEN

THE MINOAN LEGACY

T he greatest desire of any historian must surely be to travel back in time to observe at first hand those cultures that he has studied so assiduously from a distance. Only in this way could he be absolutely certain that the existing documents, surviving traditions and the archaeological record together present an accurate picture of the past. Alas, time-travel is not yet possible and we have to rely on the careful piecing together of such information as can be discovered. The further back in time the historian chooses to look, the more difficult the process becomes; the more ancient the object of his interest, the fewer the sources of information, until eventually there is no written evidence that can be easily understood and precious few artefacts to shed light on the lives of people who lived many thousands of years ago. And so in the end it comes down to interpretation.

Travelling along the tortuous mountain roads in modern Crete, looking down on sleepy villages far below, with lush crops on every side and shady olive groves, it is easy to impose late twentieth-century values and prejudices on a culture that lived here so long ago. There is a tendency for us to view such an ancient culture as 'alien' if there is a conflict between the evidence and our modern values. To remain objective is not always easy but without objectivity we have only idle speculation with no foundation to support it. The Minoan civilisation was a civilisation quite unlike any other before or since. The archaeological record shows that these were peaceful people. There is no evidence of civil insurrection during the whole of the Minoan period. Inevitably, natural catastrophes played a significant part in the history of the

Minoans because Crete is in an area of active volcanoes and where earthquakes are common. When a building was destroyed, the Minoans seem to have used this as an opportunity to build a more spectacular replacement. Artisans flourished. Trade flourished. There is little or no evidence of malnutrition, cruelty or oppression so that even to have been a slave in Minoan Crete may have been relatively comfortable. Civilisations rise and fall and the Minoan civilisation was no exception. Around 1450 BC the Minoan civilisation came to an end.

The Minoans developed an interest in astronomy and mathematics. Sometime around 2000 BC their observations led to the identification of 12 groups of stars that we now know as the zodiac. Having divided the sky into these groups, they went on to devise a calendar and a measurement system that appear to have been unique and which although altered has survived to the present day. Central to this system was a form of geometry based on a 366-degree circle; 366 was also the number of days in the Minoan year. This afforded Minoan mathematicians the means to divide the circumference of the Earth into manageable units and led to a measuring system which was in use all over megalithic Europe for many centuries.

The Minoans were fascinated by numbers, and especially by the number 4. It was with this number and its multiples that they were able to subdivide the year. Each Minoan Cycle lasted 40 years of 366 days and there were 12 of these in the Grand Cycle, which saw certain astronomical phenomena coming full circle. It must also have been obvious to them that the relative angular positions of the Sun, Mercury and Venus were replicated exactly 40 days prior to the end of each Minoan Cycle. It seems likely that they understood not only the tropical year but also the sidereal year. Observations which were almost certainly made with some form of telescope afforded them a good working knowledge of all the planets out as far as Saturn. They knew something of the distribution of mass within the solar system and noted the major moons of Mars, Jupiter and Saturn as well as Saturn's ring system. They were also aware that Jupiter and Saturn together contain most of the mass of the solar system outside of the Sun and reflected the movements of these super-giants in their mythology.

Astronomical observations and the mathematics allowed them

to develop a good navigational system so that Minoan ships would sail to destinations far beyond the eastern Mediterranean. Minoan ships may well have sailed as far west as Britain and Ireland on a regular basis.

At some time around 1450 BC, a natural disaster seems to have overtaken the civilisation. This could well have been a volcanic eruption on the nearby island of Santorini. After this, the Mycenaeans took control of the island. Minoan engineers and artists continued to ply their trade on the mainland and they did much to assist in the rise of the more warlike Mycenaean culture. Some of the population of Minoan Crete at this time may also have decided to travel to other countries, leading to the spreading of Minoan beliefs to other peoples, though their astronomy does not appear to have survived intact.

The anomalies in the present version of the measurement of space, time and geographical distance come to us courtesy of the classical Greeks who absorbed aspects of Minoan thinking but based their geometry on the Egyptian model which used a 360-degree rather than a 366-degree circle. Thus the connection between the length of year and the number of degrees in a circle was lost. This meant that time, space and geometry were no longer related as they once had been.

The Minoans may well have relied on a complex oral culture to pass information from one generation to the next. Much symbolic and mathematical information was recorded on discs incised with spirals: a design which may already have had a sacred significance that went back to neolithic times; it is found all over Western Europe. Although legend seems to indicate that there were many discs at one time, only one example has ever been found in the ruins of the Minoan civilisation. For the first time in 4,000 years, we can understand this disc, at least in part. This simple flattened ball of clay may revolutionise our understanding of Bronze Age capabilities and make us look with new eyes at parts of our own scientific heritage. Such is the accuracy of the calculations that can be performed with the numbers on this disc and so well do the numbers and the calculations fit into the complexities of the Earth and the solar system that I am certain that the numbers involved were not chosen by chance. They were chosen deliberately. It is called the Phaistos Disc.

This is my view of the Minoan civilisation, the first European super-culture to have developed.

There is a passage in *The White Goddess* which is an appropriate conclusion to this controversial study of the Phaistos Disc:

> The proleptic or analeptic method of thought, though
> necessary to poets, physicians, historians and the rest, is
> so easily confused with mere guessing, or deduction
> from insufficient data, that few of them own to using it.
> However securely I buttress the arguments of this book
> with quotations, citations and footnotes, the admission
> that I have made here of how it first came to me will
> debar it from consideration by orthodox scholars: though
> they cannot refute it, they dare not accept it.

AFTERTHOUGHTS

W hen any book is published there is always a delay between the writing and publication. Reading through the proofs of *The Bronze Age Computer Disc*, it struck me that some aspects of my subsequent research relate specifically to the thought processes in this book.

For example, I am now convinced that the mathematical corrections necessary to bring the 366-day Minoan or megalithic year into true harmony with the real Earth year were probably far less complicated than I originally believed. All that is required to achieve a staggeringly accurate year is to remove one day from the civil 366-day calendar after the completion of four 123-day cycles (492 days). I now believe that the Minoan mathematicians were primarily concerned with the sidereal Earth year and this simple expedient would have ensured that the Minoan or megalithic calendar would stay in conformity with the real sidereal year to an accuracy of less than 26 modern seconds of time within a year. As long as the tracking was for the sidereal and not the tropical year, no other compensation would have been necessary for well over 3,000 years – a stunning achievement for any culture, and incredibly accurate for a system that evolved over 5,000 years ago.

The reader will also recall the fact that I was the first to recognise the connection between Professor Thom's megalithic yard and the Minoan foot, discovered by Professor J. Walter Graham. I explored the small discrepancy between the two systems of measurement and proposed a slightly alternative world view for the megalithic peoples of Western Europe and for the Minoans, which would have been the inevitable result of such discrepancies.

It is arguable that I overstated the case in this regard. The difference between 366 megalithic yards at 82.96656 centimetres and 1,000 Minoan feet at 30.36 cm is 5.76 centimetres, measured over 303 metres. If the Minoan engineers had intended 1,000 Minoan feet to exactly equal 366 megalithic yards, then each Minoan foot would have measured 30.3657 cm, a discrepancy from Graham's findings of 0.0057 centimetres. Professor Graham had no wall longer than 170 Minoan feet with which to gain a true appreciation of the Minoan foot and most of his examples were much less. It therefore seems likely that Minoan engineers fully intended 1,000 Minoan feet to equal 366 megalithic yards and that either they, or Professor Graham, got things slightly wrong. If the latter were true, this would be entirely understandable. Archaeological ruins are immensely difficult to measure accurately and Professor Graham had far fewer examples to work with than did Professor Thom with the megalithic yard. I am now inclined to conclude that the Minoan foot is a metrication of the megalithic system and was probably retained purely for use in domestic architecture.

Why this should be the case is something of a mystery, but it is possible that the megalithic yard was uncomfortably large for such requirements and that, being a standard 40 megalithic inches in length, it was impossible to split into three equal units. However, I am firmly of the opinion that the Minoan foot, retained by the Mycenaeans and later the Greeks, was the basis of our present foot. The difference between the slightly amended Minoan foot I suggest here and the standard foot, used for so long in Britain, is about 1 mm. Readers may drawn their own conclusion about this relationship, though as I write these words I am looking at the size of 1 mm and remain staggered that any measurement so incredibly close to the Minoan foot could have survived for so long without being related back to similar ancient measurements.

The fact that 366 megalithic yards equals 1,000 Minoan feet and that this extent is a logical subdivision of the Earth's circumference seems to add credence to both Thom's and Graham's findings. The common heritage of these measuring systems, resolvable at one Minoan second of arc (polar), also supports the notion of the 366-degree circle.

Having established these facts, it is now more obvious than ever that the megalithic measurements must have come first, in order to be altered in this way by the Minoans. Megalithic monuments based on the megalithic yard are known to date from before 3000 BC, built at a time when no civilisation worthy of the name existed in Crete. How and why this mathematical system evolved is beyond the present scope of this book, but certain facts regarding its evolution are pertinent here because they stand as incontrovertible evidence of the existence of an entire system of mathematics, now sadly lost. These facts, without any manipulation on my part, lead to certain inevitable conclusions regarding the mathematical knowledge of those who created the megalithic yard. Professor Thom declared the megalithic yard to have been 2.722 feet in length, which is 82.96656 centimetres. To retain any sense of scientific credibility and yet to recognise exactly what these distant relatives of ours were capable of achieving has at times seemed difficult. However, I believe that the figures speak for themselves and the possibility of them standing up so well by pure chance is, I think, absurd. What is more, we can extrapolate from these figures a world view and an understanding of mathematics that is positively staggering when we consider the general opinions of historians regarding the capabilities of megalithic peoples.

Another aspect of this knowledge is the problem of a world that is not a true sphere, and the difficulties this could offer to any mathematician wishing to be absolutely accurate in an assessment of distances across the Earth's surface. The Earth is fatter around the equator than it is around the poles. The difference is minimal, amounting to an extra 1/600 of the polar circumference – so small, in fact, that we rarely even bother to address it, so to assume that people living 5,000 years ago could do so takes some swallowing. All I can do is to present the facts and allow readers to come to their own conclusions.

The unit of measurement I chose to call the megalithic mile is equal to 366 megalithic yards multiplied by six Minoan seconds of arc (polar Earth circumference), for I am now certain that to the Minoans there were six seconds to the minute of arc. The megalithic mile therefore equals 1.821945 kilometres. The difference between the Earth's polar circumference and the Earth's equatorial circumference is 36.6 megalithic miles, a calculation that can be confirmed by calculating the polar circumference of the Earth, which is 21,960 megalithic miles, $\frac{1}{600}$ of which is 36.6 megalithic miles.

An awareness of this fact seems to have gone into the evolution of the linear measuring system, and this occurred for a special set of reasons. Exactly why this should be of such importance only becomes apparent if the observer has some idea of the way trigonometry works. It is via trigonometry, supposedly first conceived by the ancient Greeks living in Alexandria, that it becomes possible to ascertain the circumference of the Earth at any latitude. Trigonometry works by using mathematical laws relating right-angled triangles to the measurement of circles and spheres. The astonishing thing about Minoan, and by implication megalithic, mathematics is that trigonometry does not have to be applied to them at all, for it is built into the system as part of its working matrix.

For example: if I wish to calculate the circumference of the Earth at any given latitude, for example 40° north or south of the equator, I would approach this problem by first establishing the cosine for 40°. This is a painless process these days thanks to scientific calculators, although before their invention, I only needed to consult a book of mathematical tables. The cosine for 40° is 0.76604444311. I simply multiply this figure by the equatorial circumference of the Earth to establish the circumference at 40°. Using an equatorial circumference of 21,960 megalithic miles, the result is 16,822.335 megalithic miles.

But there is a fascinating fact here that I discovered quite early in my research. The distance across 1'M of arc at 40° latitude when expressed in megalithic miles is 0.76604444311, exactly the same number as the cosine for 40°. What is more, if we turn this figure into megalithic yards, 1,682.233, and then move the decimal point one digit to the right, to give 16,822.3, we have established the circumference of the Earth at 40° latitude in megalithic miles, simply by looking at the distance across one Minoan minute of arc. Professional mathematicians and engineers have found these mathematical shortcuts surprising in the extreme, and they can only work because of the number bases chosen for the whole system in the first place.

What is more, things go further than this. It seemed to me impossible to believe that it is a mere chance that the difference between polar Earth circumference and equatorial Earth circumference is 36.6 megalithic miles. We have seen time and again just how important the number 366 is to the whole Minoan and megalithic principle, and here it is echoed again. In fact, its existence provides us with a lightning-quick method of dealing with the difference between polar and equatorial Earth circumferences and is a means of establishing the actual distance between any two points on the Earth's surface with stunning accuracy. In other words, the whole system was created with the difference between these circumference measurements in mind.

It has taken six years to realise fully all that is written in these pages, and yet once I understood the concepts the world exploded for me into a series of discoveries and a development of understanding that would never have been possible if the Phaistos Disc had not come first. I now know that these principles certainly did not die when the last megalithic monument was dragged into place or when the volcano on Santorini engulfed Crete with its volcanic ash, and my researches are still continuing.

In the early years of the twentieth century, an archaeologist crouched, staring in the light of a flickering candle into the receding blackness of a tomb that had been sealed for thousands of years. His rich patron, stunned by the silence or the force of an indrawn breath that he could not interpret, asked:

'Well! Can you see anything?'

I feel like that archaeologist, because this first glimpse at the sheer brilliance of the minds that invented the most perfect mathematical principle the world has ever known has opened up vistas that none of us had even imagined and which only make sense in the light of the megalithic mathematical principles. Many of these subsequent historical discoveries and realisations are, as I write these words, within my sight. And as you, the reader, strain to peer over my shoulder, you too may ask:

'Well Alan! Can you see anything?'

And, like that archaeologist, for the moment I can only say, inadequately,

'Oh yes! Wonderful things!'

MINOAN MEASUREMENTS
AND MODERN EQUIVALENTS
REFERENCE CHART

1 Minoan second

= 1,000 Minoan feet

= ⅙ of a Minoan minute of the Earth's circumference

In modern time = 0.6557 seconds standard mean solar day

In modern distance = 996.06 imperial feet = 303.6 metres

1 Minoan minute

= 6,000 Minoan feet

= 1 Minoan mile

= ¹⁄₆₀ of a Minoan degree of the Earth's circumference

In modern time = 3.93442623 seconds standard mean solar day

In modern distance = 1.13189 miles = 1.8216 kilometres

1 Minoan degree

= 60 Minoan miles

= 360,000 Minoan feet

= ¹⁄₃₆₆ of Earth's estimated circumference

In modern time = 3.9442623 seconds standard mean solar day

In modern distance = 67.9134 miles = 109.296 kilometres

1 Minoan hour

(All mean averages alternate 30 and 31 degree signs)

= 1 zodiac sign

= 10,980,000 Minoan feet

= 1,830 Minoan miles

= ¹⁄₁₂ (average) of Earth's estimated circumference

In modern time = 120 minutes standard mean solar day

In modern distance = 2,071.3587 miles = 3,333.528 kilometres

The Minoan circle

= 366 Minoan degrees

= 131,760,000 Minoan feet

= 21,960 Minoan miles

In modern time = 24 hours standard mean solar day

In modern distance = 24,856.3044 miles = 40,002.336 kilometres

THE MINOAN FOOT AND MEGALITHIC EQUIVALENTS REFERENCE CHART

1 Minoan foot = 0.3659 megalithic yards
1 Minoan foot = 14.752 megalithic inches

100 Minoan feet = 36.593 megalithic yards
100 Minoan feet = 1,463.725 megalithic inches

1,000 Minoan feet = 365.93 megalithic yards
1,000 Minoan feet = 14,637.25 megalithic inches

BIBLIOGRAPHY

Adamson, David, *The Ruins of Time*, Allen & Unwin, 1975

Alcock, Leslie, *Arthur's Britain*, Penguin, 1971

Atkinson, R. J. C., *Stonehenge*, Harmondsworth, 1960

Bhakitivedanta, A. C., *Bhagavad-cita As It Is*, Bhakitivedanta Book Trust, 1968

Bronowski, J., *The Ascent of Man*, BBC, 1973

Budlong, John P., *Sky and Sextant*

Charroux, Robert, *Lost Worlds*, Editions Robert Laffont, 1971

Cottrel, Leonard, *The Bull of Minos*, Pan Books Ltd, 1965

de Camp, L. Sprague and Catherine C., *Citadels of Mystery*, Souvenir Press, 1965

Doumas, Christos G., *Santorini*, Hannibal, Athens.

Dyer, James, *Discovering Archaeology in Denmark*, Shire Publications, 1972

Gale, Mort, *Moonpower*, Warner Books, 1980

Gantz, Jeffrey, *The Mabinogion*, Penguin, 1976

Graves, Robert, *The White Goddess*, Faber & Faber, 1961

Green, Roger Lancelyn, *Myths of the Norsemen*, Penguin, 1970

Gribbin, John and Stephen Plageman, *The Jupiter Effect*, Macmillan Press, 1974

Hadingham, Evan, *Circles and Standing Stones*, London, 1975

Hawkes, Jacquetta, *Dawn of the Gods*, Chatto & Windus, 1968

Hawkins, Gerald S., *Stonehenge Decoded*, Souvenir Press, 1966

Henshaw, Audrey, *The Chambered Tombs of Scotland* (2 volumes), Edinburgh, 1963 and 1972

Hesiod, *Hesiod and Theognis,* Penguin Classics, 1973

Homer, *Iliad*, Penguin, 1950

Irwin, Keith G., *The 365 Days*, George Harrap, 1965

Kean, Victor J., *Crete: New Light on Old Mysteries,* Efstathiadis Group, 1993

Kerenyi, Carl, *The Gods of the Greeks*, Thames & Hudson, 1951

Jackson, Anthony, *The Symbol Stones of Scotland*, The Orkney Press, 1987

Laing, Lloyd and Jennifer, *The Origins of Britain*, Routledge & Kegan Paul, 1980

Mackie, Euan, *The Megalith Builders*, Phaidon Press, 1977

Mackie, Euan, *Science and Society in Prehistoric Britain*, London, 1977

Mathioulakis, Chr. Z., *Knossos*, Chr. Z. Mathioulakis.

Noblecourt, Christian Desroches, *Tutankhamen*, Michael Joseph, 1963

Norwich, John Julius, *Byzantium*, Guild Publishing, 1989

Phillips, Guy Ragland, *Brigantia*, Routledge & Kegan Paul, 1976

Piggot, S., *The Druids*, Thames & Hudson, 1968

Piggot, S., *Neolithic Cultures of the British Isles*, Cambridge, 1954

Playfair, Guy Lyon and Scott Hill, *The Cycles of Heaven*, Souvenir Press, 1978

Rothes, Gunter D., *Handbook of Planet Observers*

Sambursky, *The Physical World of the Greeks*, Routledge, 1956

San Thomas, Domingo de, *The Lexicon*

Sandars, N. K., *The Sea Peoples*, Thames & Hudson, 1978

Schele, Linda and David Friedel, *A Forest of Kings,* William Morrow, New York, 1990

Schultz, Joachim, *Movement and Rhythms of the Stars*, Floris Books, 1986

Seymour, Dr Percy, *Astrology, The Evidence of Science*, Lennard Publishing, 1988

Streatfield, Noel, *The Boy Pharaoh, Tutankhamen*, Michael Joseph, 1972

Sturluson, Snorri, *Prose Edda*

Stylianos, Alexiou, *Minoan Civilisation* Spyros Alexiou & Sons, Heraclion

Swift, Jonathan, *Gulliver's Travels*

Thom, A., *Megalithic Sites in Britain*, Oxford, 1967

Thom, A. and A. S., *Megalithic Remains in Britain and Brittany*, OUP, 1978

Vandenabeele, Frieda, *Malia*, Ekidotike Athenon S A, Athens, 1992

Vassilakis, Antonis (translated by Alexandra Doumas), *Phaistos*,
I. Mathioulakis, Athens

von Daniken, Erich, *Chariots of the Gods?*, Souvenir Press, 1969

Warren, Peter, *The Aegean Civilisations*, Equinox (Oxford), 1975

Wilcock, John and Pepper, Elizabeth, *Magical and Mystical Sites*,
Abacus, 1978

Wunderlich, H. G., *The Secret of Crete*, Souvenir Press, 1975

INDEX